BOOK OF MORMON
STUDIES

BOOK OF MORMON STUDIES

AN INTRODUCTION AND GUIDE

Daniel Becerra | Amy Easton-Flake
Nicholas J. Frederick | Joseph M. Spencer

Published by the Religious Studies Center, Brigham Young University, Provo, Utah, in cooperation with Deseret Book Company, Salt Lake City.
Visit us at rsc.byu.edu.

© 2022 by Brigham Young University. All rights reserved.

Printed in the United States of America by Sheridan Books, Inc.

DESERET BOOK is a registered trademark of Deseret Book Company.
Visit us at DeseretBook.com.

Any uses of this material beyond those allowed by the exemptions in US copyright law, such as section 107, "Fair Use," and section 108, "Library Copying," require the written permission of the publisher, Religious Studies Center, 185 HGB, Brigham Young University, Provo, UT 84602. The views expressed herein are the responsibility of the authors and do not necessarily represent the position of Brigham Young University or the Religious Studies Center.

Cover and interior design by Carmen Durland Cole
Cover image courtesy of Gerrit J. Dirkmaat

Hardcover ISBN: 978-1-9503-0426-4
Paperback ISBN: 978-1-9503-0429-5

Library of Congress Cataloging-in-Publication Data

Names: Becerra, Daniel, 1985– author. | Easton-Flake, Amy A., author. | Frederick, Nicholas J., author. | Spencer, Joseph M., author.
Title: Book of Mormon studies : an introduction and guide / Daniel Becerra, Amy Easton-Flake, Nicholas J. Frederick, Joseph M. Spencer.
Description: Provo, Utah : Religious Studies Center, Brigham Young University : Salt Lake City, Utah : Deseret Book, [2022] | Includes bibliographical references and index. | Summary: "Where does one go to learn more about Book of Mormon studies? For those who do not regularly engage with scholarship, it's hard to know how to begin. Currently there's no general guide to Book of Mormon scholarship available to the public. Given all that's happened in the last few decades-and especially all that's happening right now-in Book of Mormon studies, this situation needs to be remedied. This introduction breaks down Book of Mormon studies, from its history to the obstacles that will need to be overcome as it moves forward. Additionally, this introduction provides readers with resources that they can turn to for further information on Book of Mormon studies"—Provided by publisher.
Identifiers: LCCN 2021045707 | ISBN 9781950304264 (hardcover)
Subjects: LCSH: Book of Mormon—Criticism, interpretation, etc. | Book of Mormon—Criticism, interpretation, etc.—History. | Book of Mormon—Authorship. | Book of Mormon—History.
Classification: LCC BX8627 .B325 2022 | DDC 289.3/22—dc23/eng/20211202
LC record available at https://lccn.loc.gov/2021045707

Contents

vii
Acknowledgments

1
Introduction

11
Chapter 1: Looking Back

31
Chapter 2: The Field

63
Chapter 3: Overcoming Obstacles

83
Chapter 4: Common Questions

109
Chapter 5: New Directions

127
Conclusion

131
Appendix

165
Index

175
About the Authors

Acknowledgments

The authors wish to thank, first, the able research assistants who helped make this project come to fruition: Alice Judd and Sydney Ballif. Sydney in particular helped shape the use of graphics throughout the book. We're very grateful to Julie Frederick, who read the manuscript with great care and made the book much better than it would be. As the director of publications at the Religious Studies Center when this project began, Scott Esplin championed it from the beginning. It owes much to his encouragement. We're grateful to reviewers of the manuscript throughout the publication process, who gave helpful feedback and valuable suggestions. Jared W. Ludlow, Joany O. Pinegar, Brent R. Nordgren, Julie Newman, Carmen D. Cole, and Myla Parke at the Religious Studies Center did impressive work on bringing the book to life. Their expertise is something we appreciate greatly.

Finally, we wish to thank Frank Judd, our colleague in the Department of Ancient Scripture, for his encouragement to undertake this project. It was due to his excitement that we decided to take what was just an idea and make it a reality.

Introduction

Latter-day Saints take the Book of Mormon seriously. They read and study it, memorize its passages, and mark up its pages. Individuals and families make it the center of their devotional study as they seek God's voice in its pages and search it for answers to hard questions. Missionaries consume it, sifting its stories and sermons so they can teach with conviction. Quoted over the pulpit and mentioned in personal conversations, studied in pricey leather-bound editions and read on flickering phone screens, the Book of Mormon is ubiquitous in the life of the Saints. It's so ubiquitous, in fact, that members of the Church sometimes reach a saturation point. Some stories and sermons may become *too* familiar and, as a consequence, can lose some of their vitality and power. "I already know this," many find themselves saying as they read. "Is there something more to learn here? Should I be studying something else?"

This is a wholly understandable but also a lamentable feeling. It's lamentable not only because the Book of Mormon is an infinitely rich text, filled with the Spirit of God and equipped to exalt those who abide by its precepts, but also because the familiarity many feel can be a superficial one. That is, people are often familiar with only one or two layers

Introduction

of the text. Thus it isn't the Book of Mormon but the way in which one studies it that can limit its potential to inform and transform the reader. Perhaps we're led to think we know the book so well because we don't know how to reveal its real riches and depths. There are more resources available today for studying the Book of Mormon seriously than ever before. In fact, we seem to be at the beginning of a golden age of Book of Mormon scholarship, but the good work that's going on isn't reaching most Latter-day Saints.

The last half century or so has seen a rather general flowering of Latter-day Saint intellectual culture. Particularly productive has been the field of Latter-day Saint history, which has recently come to be a recognized field of scholarship in the larger academy. Going by the name of "Mormon studies" nowadays, this field has traditionally included within it scholarship on the Book of Mormon. For most of the short history of Mormon studies, however, scholarship on the Book of Mormon has been treated as something primarily if not exclusively for religious insiders. In part, this is because so much scholarship on the Book of Mormon in the twentieth century was explicitly produced in the hope of either defending or attacking the faith claims (the beliefs) of The Church of Jesus Christ of Latter-day Saints. The field of Mormon studies has long been inhabited, however, by a spirit of neutrality with respect to faith claims. But something interesting has begun to happen in recent years. Book of Mormon scholarship that draws a broader audience has begun to appear, demanding attention from scholars outside the faith tradition and built on the idea that the Book of Mormon deserves to be studied in its own right—and not just for the purposes of defending or attacking the Church. In the context of these developments, scholarly work on the Book of Mormon has expanded dramatically, both in content and in scope. There's much going on, and it can be difficult to know how to find one's way around the field.

It's also worth saying that Book of Mormon studies can be a fraught place to work. The Book of Mormon is sacred scripture for Latter-day Saints, and research methods originally forged in the secular academy

> It isn't the Book of Mormon but the way in which one studies it that can limit its potential to inform and transform the reader.

Introduction

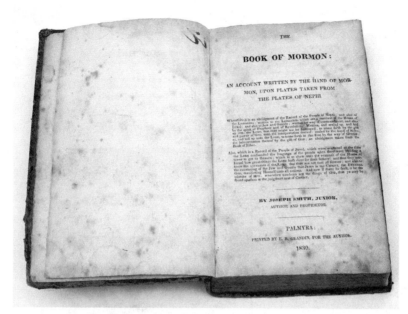

The title page of the 1830 edition of the Book of Mormon. Courtesy of Intellectual Reserve, Inc.

might seem like dangerous things to bring to the task of studying such a thing. It is certainly true that the history of Book of Mormon studies has featured a good many controversies and a lot of wrangling. Feelings rightly run high when our deepest convictions are concerned. In our view, it's crucial to recognize this engagement outright. There are real dangers involved in Book of Mormon studies. There's also, though, a great deal of promise. What's needed is a wise approach to serious study of the Book of Mormon, one attentive to the concrete concerns of devoted believers. How can one balance a real recognition of the good that scholarship can do with a healthy skepticism about just how far scholarship can go? Negotiating the field of Book of Mormon studies isn't just a matter of knowing what's out there, nor of getting a list of safe books and articles to read, things beyond reproach. It requires developing real wisdom about what's to be learned from all that's going on in the field—and about what calls for caution.

For all these reasons, we've felt like it would be valuable to produce a short, readable introduction to Book of Mormon studies. For those

Introduction

A first-edition Book of Mormon, printed in 1830. Courtesy of Intellectual Reserve, Inc.

who do not regularly engage with scholarship, it's hard to know how to begin. Where do you find the important articles and books? Which sources provide reliable answers to hard questions? How does one know what the different schools of thought are? What challenges does one face in entering the field of Book of Mormon studies, even as a reader? These are the questions we try to answer in the following pages. The four of us who have contributed to this book are all religious educators at Brigham Young University (BYU) and are avid participants in the field of Book of Mormon studies. We write and publish for interested lay Latter-day Saint readers but also for scholarly audiences. We lecture to other academics using theory-laden language and multisyllabic adjectives at large conferences, but we also talk like normal human beings with our fellow believers in our classrooms at BYU. In this book, we try to bridge the unfortunate gap that often exists between the two worlds we inhabit all the time.

Currently there's no general guide to Book of Mormon scholarship available to the public. While some bibliographies and reviews of literature on specific topics are scattered about, few know where to find them. Internet searches are unfortunately unreliable, and the online resources that currently exist generally provide little context and so don't tend to help the uninitiated get their bearings. Given all that's happened in the last few decades—and especially all that's happening right now—in Book of Mormon studies, this situation needs to be remedied. Introductory guides exist for almost every field of scholarship and are generally updated every few years to keep things current. Book of Mormon studies has grown to the point that it needs such an introductory guide, and so we want to provide one for those who are interested in engaging with the Book of Mormon in a more scholarly way. We recognize from the outset that what we're putting together has its limitations and will require regular revising and updating. But we also know that things have to start somewhere, and we want to get things started.

We imagine three different kinds of readers picking up this book, and we've made efforts to engage all of them. First and above all, we want to write to believing Latter-day Saints—especially young ones—who are interested in contributing to Book of Mormon scholarship. We thus hope this book provides much-needed orientation for budding Book of Mormon scholars and that it might inspire others who are merely curious to try their hand at Book of Mormon scholarship. Second, though, we write also for the many Latter-day Saints who we know want to deepen their private study of the Book of Mormon without any ambitions about producing new scholarship. These readers might turn to a book like this for help in navigating their way through the growing body of Book of Mormon scholarship. And so we hope that this book helps direct such readers to the best of what's happened and what's happening and that it provides them with enough context to read sometimes difficult scholarship comfortably and with appropriate caution. Third and most delicately, we write for non–Latter-day Saint scholars (and nonscholars) who have some interest in the Book of Mormon and might appreciate some guidance in navigating a field that's so deeply shaped by the concerns of believing readers. Although we haven't written this book in the aspiringly neutral tone of the academy, we hope it will nonetheless serve such readers too, helping them sort out the field despite our efforts to speak principally to those within the faith.

Now, what's the shape of the book you hold in your hands? Our presentation of the field is relatively simple. The first chapter provides a broad sketch of the history of Book of Mormon studies, tracing that history from the beginning all the way to the rapid expansion of the field in recent years. The second chapter, somewhat longer, surveys the field as it's now constituted, explaining its seven subdisciplines by providing background and identifying major contributions. In the third chapter, we talk about important obstacles that need to be overcome as the field of Book of Mormon studies moves forward. Then the fourth and fifth chapters clarify what overcoming those obstacles really looks like. A short conclusion follows.

At the end of the book is an appendix of a more practical nature. Its aim is to provide simple information about what interested readers might turn to next after reading this introduction to Book of Mormon studies. Publication information for the works mentioned throughout this book can be found in the appendix. The appendix goes much further than just providing full citations, however. It is divided into five parts. The principal audience of the first part ("Getting Started") is the average Latter-day Saint rather than the budding scholar. It lays out the first steps to take in drawing on the very best of Book of Mormon scholarship for personal or devotional study. The second part ("Getting Serious") is instead for the budding Book of Mormon scholar, someone hoping to know the field better. It gathers full citation information for books and essays mentioned throughout the book that anyone working in the field of Book of Mormon studies should know. It also includes brief annotations to help the student find her or his way. The third part

Introduction

> **AN OVERVIEW OF THE CHAPTERS WITHIN THIS BOOK**
>
> | | |
> |---|---|
> | Chapter 1 | History of the field of Book of Mormon studies, from the first scholarly investigations of the Book of Mormon to the end of the twentieth century |
> | Chapter 2 | Shape of the field today, divided into seven subdisciplines (production of the text, historical origins, literary criticism, intertextual study, theological interpretation, reception history, and ideology critique) |
> | Chapter 3 | Obstacles to be overcome for the field's long-term success |
> | Chapter 4 | Questions traditionally addressed in Book of Mormon studies (How was the book translated? How do we explain changes to the text? What sources might lie behind the text? What of anachronisms in the text? Should language from Isaiah be in the Book of Mormon? What of New Testament language in the volume? Where did the Book of Mormon take place?) |
> | Chapter 5 | Questions being addressed today in Book of Mormon studies (How do we make sense of race in the Book of Mormon? Why are there so few women in the volume? How should we approach war and violence in the text? How relevant is the book in the twenty-first century?) |

("Getting Specialized") gets still more detailed and is aimed at students interested in specific topics. It notes books and articles mentioned throughout the text on specialized topics and includes (still briefer) annotations. The fourth part ("Getting Around") is again aimed at all readers. It identifies and briefly discusses the major journals, book publishers, research outfits, and other institutions that are important to Book of Mormon studies. The fifth part is a list of other works we've cited along the way. What's gathered in this appendix is of course anything but exhaustive, but it's meant to be a relatively comprehensive guide to the most important work in Book of Mormon studies.

One last question: Why us? Who are we? And why does it take four people to write a short book like this? As we've mentioned, we're religious educators at BYU, professors who teach and write professionally about the Book of Mormon, among other things, for a living. Although we're all relatively young, we've collectively written six books and over fifty

Introduction

> **QUESTIONS ANSWERED IN THE APPENDIX**
>
> Part 1 — Which edition of the Book of Mormon is most useful? What is the best introductory source on the story of the book's coming forth? Where can one read about the history of the book's reception? Are there any books on the Book of Mormon that everyone should read?
>
> Part 2 — Are there other editions of the Book of Mormon one should consider? What are the standard reference materials in Book of Mormon studies? Where can one find bibliographies and literature reviews for the field? Are there more specialized publications on the history of the Book of Mormon's reception? What classic studies of the Book of Mormon are scholars who are working in the field expected to know? What more recent works should anyone getting serious about the field read?
>
> Part 3 — What if someone wants to get much more into the weeds in Book of Mormon studies? What might she or he read?
>
> Part 4 — What scholarly journals and presses publish work on the Book of Mormon? Are there online resources for Book of Mormon studies? Are there regular conferences on the Book of Mormon? What other institutions exist that sponsor research on the Book of Mormon?
>
> Part 5 — Where can someone find full citation information for any other sources that we've mentioned along the way?

articles and book chapters on the Book of Mormon (with many more on the way). We've all presented numerous papers on the Book of Mormon at conferences and taught dozens of courses on the Book of Mormon at BYU. In our ranks are editors and associate editors of the *Journal of Book of Mormon Studies*, officers of the Book of Mormon Studies Association, members of the Book of Mormon Academy, editors of and contributors to *The Book of Mormon: Brief Theological Introductions*, hosts of and participants in televised and online reflections on the Book of Mormon, and scholars writing about the Book of Mormon for major non–Latter-day Saint publishing outlets. Each of us brings devoted years of time, study, and research to this book.

Really, any of us might have written this book individually. We recognize, though, that a book that covers so many different areas and wrestles with so many important issues would suffer from being limited to one perspective. Each of us comes from different fields of study. Professor Becerra was trained in early Christian history at Duke University, Professor Easton-Flake in American literature at Brandeis University, Professor Frederick in Mormon studies at Claremont Graduate University, and Professor Spencer in philosophy at the University of New Mexico. Each of us, moreover, brings a different area of interest or specialization to the Book of Mormon: ethics (Professor Becerra), literary studies (Professor Easton-Flake), intertextuality (Professor Frederick), and theology (Professor Spencer). The diversity among our interests, backgrounds, and positions is, despite its still very real limits, an asset in trying to sketch the shape of the field we all work in.

One thing we certainly share is love for and devotion to the study of the Book of Mormon. We believe the Book of Mormon can thrive in both devotional and academic settings, and we hope our efforts here help it do so.[1]

NOTE

1. In many ways, the present book began as a much-shorter article written by two of us—Professors Frederick and Spencer—and published in the *Religious Educator* in 2020. In what follows, we've taken the liberty of drawing passages from that article on occasion. We thank the *Religious Educator* for allowing us to reprint that material.

| CHAPTER 1 |

Looking Back

When and how did the field of Book of Mormon studies begin? Was there a specific moment when it decisively started or an identifiable event that inaugurated it? When did it begin to differentiate itself from devotional reflection on the text? Is there a story to be told about the field's history, about changing trends or periods in which specific kinds of research prevailed? These aren't idle questions. As is so often the case for scholarly disciplines, knowing the backstory behind today's field of Book of Mormon studies is immensely helpful. It clarifies the stakes of current controversies within the field, and it explains why it's easier to find scholarship on certain issues and harder to find scholarship on others. It's also—at least, for those of us working in the field—simply interesting in its own right.

How did things look for the Book of Mormon right at the start of the Restoration? Well, scholars have long claimed that Latter-day Saints didn't pay much attention to the Book of Mormon before the twentieth century. And it's certainly true that early Church-published periodicals and recorded sermons from Church leaders quoted from the Bible more often than from the Book of Mormon. Called on to speak

> "Looking at the Book of Mormon in terms of its early uses and reception, it becomes clear that this American scripture has exerted influence within the church and reaction outside the church not primarily by virtue of its substance, but rather its manner of appearing, not on the merits of what it says, but what it enacts."
>
> —Terryl Givens, *By the Hand of Mormon: The American Scripture That Launched a New World Religion*

or write for the public, one naturally turns to the familiar, and the Bible was more familiar to the first generation or two of Saints than the Book of Mormon was. More recent scholarship, however, has labored to show that the earliest Saints valued the Book of Mormon in their personal devotional worship. Members of the Church read the book carefully, letting it shape their religious and social worlds.[1] Thus, for individuals engaged with the Book of Mormon, the first decades of the Church's history were mostly a period of growing familiarity—gained through devoted study and practical-minded reading. It naturally took a generation or two for the book to become a regular resource for scholarly study. But by the end of the nineteenth century, the Book of Mormon was ready to serve as the object of intellectual analysis.

It's probably wrong to describe anything before the 1940s as making up a field—even a nascent or fledgling field—of Book of Mormon studies, but there were early stirrings of great importance late in the nineteenth century. Orson Pratt, an Apostle and a self-taught intellectual, led the way. Not only did Pratt make the Book of Mormon a consistent focus in his ministry, but he also made lasting efforts to draw the Saints toward serious study of the book. Most important among these efforts was his work on the 1879 edition of the Book of Mormon. For the first half century of the Church's history, the Book of Mormon had in certain ways been printed like a novel—with long chapters and (in most editions) unnumbered paragraphs. There were no verses, no footnotes, no Bible-like double columns. As Pratt worked on the new edition—

he'd already produced groundbreaking new editions of the Doctrine and Covenants in 1876 and the Pearl of Great Price in 1878—he transformed the Book of Mormon text into a resource for study. He broke up longer chapters from earlier editions (creating the chapter divisions familiar to Latter-day Saints today), divided the text into numbered verses (the same used in the Church today), and filled the bottom of each page with notes for study (replaced with fresh notes in later editions). Pratt thus created a more citable, more researchable version of the Book of Mormon.

The new edition of the Book of Mormon opened a space for Latter-day Saints to pursue scholarly writing on the scripture. Arguably the first individual to do so was George Reynolds. Enabled by Pratt's 1879 edition, Reynolds wrote a substantial book-length study, *The Story of the Book of Mormon*, and produced both *A Dictionary of the Book of Mormon* and *A Complete Concordance to the Book of Mormon*. In these works, Reynolds attempted to sort the Book of Mormon's words and names and stories for the first time. When Reynolds died in 1909, he did so watching a new generation of readers of the Book of Mormon come into their own, building on his and Pratt's work. Work on the Book of Mormon in the first decades of the twentieth century, however, had a broader focus than Reynolds's work. Some defended the Book of Mormon's claims to inspiration and ancient historicity, such as B. H. Roberts in his three-volume *New Witnesses for God* and Janne M. Sjödahl in his

Orson Pratt. Courtesy of Wikimedia Commons.

George Reynolds. Courtesy of Intellectual Reserve, Inc.

B. H. Roberts. Courtesy of Intellectual Reserve, Inc.

Left to right: Hugh Nibley, M. Wells Jakeman, and Sidney Sperry. Photos courtesy of Neal A. Maxwell Institute for Religious Scholarship and Religious Studies Center, Brigham Young University.

Introduction to the Study of the Book of Mormon. Others laid the foundations for literary and theological work on the Book of Mormon, such as Roy A. West in *An Introduction to the Book of Mormon: A Religious-Literary Study* and William E. Berrett and Milton R. Hunter in *A Guide to the Study of the Book of Mormon*.

This same period—and the 1920s in particular—witnessed some quiet challenges for the Book of Mormon that would eventually prove deeply important. The 1920s opened with yet another new official edition of the Book of Mormon, this one the product of Elder James E. Talmage's careful work. About the time it appeared, however, a member of the Church sent to Elder Talmage a letter with a series of difficult questions about the Book of Mormon's relationship to the archaeological record. Elder Talmage assigned B. H. Roberts to work up answers to the questions, but Roberts found himself baffled and concerned by the questions rather than confidently prepared to answer them. Roberts in fact produced hundreds of pages of private notes carefully investigating the questions but came to no comforting conclusions. Roberts ultimately seemed content to let the questions be, perhaps hoping that they might remain obscure and therefore not trouble others. But the same kinds of criticisms came to public prominence in the mid-1940s when Fawn McKay Brodie published her still-popular book *No Man Knows My History: The Life of Joseph Smith*. Brodie's book was an investigative journalistic biography of Joseph Smith that presented the Book of Mormon as the product of the Prophet's synthetic genius. In making

difficult questions about the Book of Mormon a matter for public conversation rather than for private reflection, though, Brodie arguably provided the much-needed spur to create a serious (if nonetheless small) field of Book of Mormon scholarship.

More or less at the very moment that Brodie's book appeared, the first generation of university-trained scholars who could bring their skills and expertise to the study of the Book of Mormon also came on the scene. In 1946, M. Wells Jakeman, a Berkeley-trained Mesoamerican archaeologist, joined the faculty at Brigham Young University (BYU) and began to publish professionally about Book of Mormon archaeology. By the end of the decade, Jakeman was leading university-sponsored digs in Central America—in search of Book of Mormon lands while also aiming to contribute to the field of Mesoamerican anthropology. Also in 1946, hard on the heels of publishing a direct rebuttal to Brodie's book, Hugh Nibley joined the faculty at BYU and was soon hard at work on a long string of publications connecting the Book of Mormon to the world of the ancient Near East. Nibley was also trained at the University of California at Berkeley, and his specialization in ancient Old World civilizations would prove particularly influential in the ensuing years. Further, Sidney Sperry, with a doctorate in biblical literature from the University of Chicago and a position at BYU (acquired much earlier, in 1932), began writing consistently on the Book of Mormon. Sperry would give his attention in particularly acute ways to what he called "the problems of the Book of Mormon"—largely issues surrounding the Book of Mormon's relationship to the Bible.[2]

These three figures—Jakeman, Nibley, and Sperry—effectively founded Book of Mormon studies as an academic (rather than an aspiringly academic) discipline. They largely limited their intentions to intellectually defending the Book of Mormon against its critics, but they brought real training to the task and saw things in the text that previous generations of readers hadn't. Bluntly put, they provided the

Book of Mormon Studies

> "The role of personalities was easily visible at BYU where Jakeman, Sperry, and Nibley (more or less my early local mentors) couldn't agree on anything."
>
> —John L. Sorenson, "Ask the Scholar," Neal A. Maxwell Institute for Religious Scholarship

first genuinely scholarly readings of the book, bringing a new sophistication and discipline to its study. Jakeman's contribution would prove to lie principally in producing a worthy successor for himself, someone who could further his own work while putting it on a much more solid methodological foundation. Jakeman was prone to claim more than the data allowed, quick to find evidence but slow to bring a necessary critical eye to his findings. Sperry's contribution was more direct than Jakeman's—his four major books on the Book of Mormon were collectively groundbreaking—and yet his influence would prove unfortunately fleeting, his writings underappreciated after his passing. Despite people's occasional attempts at recovering his insights, Sperry's work is largely regarded today as a relic of a past era of Book of Mormon scholarship. Nibley's work on the Book of Mormon, in contrast with his two colleagues, would acquire striking longevity. All of Nibley's major works on the Book of Mormon remain available in print today and continue to shape the field well into the twenty-first century. By the end of the twentieth century—a few years before his passing—Nibley had become a living legend, his efforts at defending the Book of Mormon an example held up for imitation.

For two decades, Jakeman, Nibley, and Sperry dominated Latter-day Saint intellectual culture and gave believers reason to feel that the Book of Mormon was intellectually credible and rationally defensible. Then, however, they began all at once to retreat from Book of Mormon research. Jakeman published his last major archaeological studies connected to the Book of Mormon early in the 1960s, leaving the field of research he'd plowed to others. Sperry's crowning *Book of Mormon Compendium* appeared in 1968, after which he largely retired from the public eye, passing away just a few years later. Nibley published the last of his major books on the Book of Mormon, *Since Cumorah*, in 1967, at which point he turned his attention to other interests (principally the newly recovered papyri associated with the Book of Abraham). In many ways, it seems as if Book of Mormon scholars felt they'd had their say and had their day, and they were ready to pass the torch to others. And at that very moment a burgeoning Latter-day Saint intellectual movement was on the rise, ready to take center stage.

Attention would swing around again to the Book of Mormon a couple of decades later, but in the wake of important events. For example, led by Leonard J. Arrington, trained Latter-day Saint historians had by the mid-1960s established themselves as part of the larger historical discipline, simultaneously bringing professionalism to Latter-day Saint history and Latter-day Saint history to the profession. By the early 1970s, studying the history of the Restoration—rather than analyzing or defending scripture—had become the predominant focus of Latter-day Saint scholarship. The forward momentum of this movement (which soon came to be known as "new Mormon history") eventually faltered, however. Church leaders—who had directly sponsored much of the historical work being done—grew nervous about the movement in the late 1970s. The Church then withdrew sponsorship for various historical projects in the early 1980s. Part of what spurred this retreat from institutional support was the alarming "discovery" of historical documents that called the sacred origins of the Latter-day Saint tradition—and particularly of the Book of Mormon—into question. These documents were eventually, but only eventually, revealed to be forgeries created by Mark Hofmann. The eagerness and excitement that certain historians exhibited in studying and drawing conclusions from these documents, however, raised lasting concerns among believers about whether scholars had the wisdom to postpone drawing conclusions until the data could all be collected and contextualized thoroughly.

These developments coincided with an increase in the intensity of lay and popular religious criticism of the Church. In fact, the 1980s were difficult for conservative religions in the United States of America quite generally. Countercultural movements and popular identity politics originating in the 1960s had become part of mainstream culture by that point, and so the faith-driven conservative culture that had dominated the period immediately following World War II was increasingly marginalized and even demonized. Religion was coming to be seen as a protector of racism, sexism, classism, and homophobia. Naturally, then, the 1980s also witnessed a reaction to these developments from what was soon called "the religious right," a version of political conservatism that saw the battle for America's identity as deeply bound up with a battle over religion. Latter-day Saints in the United States found their place in this fraught religious and political conflict only uneasily. Their generally conservative views on social issues aligned them in many ways with the religious right, but the same 1980s also saw an astonishing increase in antagonism toward Latter-day Saints from conservative Christians in America. Evangelicals therefore tended to see in Latter-day Saints not potential political allies but pseudo-Christians whose marked success in global missionary work during the previous several decades was a real threat to Christianity. Latter-day Saints thus faced social and cultural marginalization on one side and sustained "anti-Mormon" campaigns on the other.

It's worth reviewing these historical and political matters between the late 1960s and the early 1980s because they unquestionably shaped the field of Book of Mormon studies when it reemerged with peculiar force. Renewed scholarly critiques of the Book of Mormon's origins and claims to antiquity, combined with antagonism from nonscholars in the larger Christian world, motivated a whole generation of young Latter-day Saint scholars to turn their attention to the Book of Mormon in the early 1980s. These scholars came to the book's defense in an organized and collaborative fash-

> **IMPORTANT DEVELOPMENTS SPURRING BOOK OF MORMON STUDIES ACTIVITY IN THE 1980S**
>
> - Mark Hofmann's forgeries raise questions about the Book of Mormon's origins in a way that contributes to a crisis among Latter-day Saint historians.
> - "Anti-Mormon" critiques of the Book of Mormon (and of related faith claims) increase at the popular level.
> - President Ezra Taft Benson gives a series of sermons endorsing a stronger devotional connection to the Book of Mormon.
> - The rise of the religious right in the United States places Latter-day Saints in an uncomfortable political position.

ion. Deepening their motivations was an increasingly felt need among Latter-day Saints in general to have the Book of Mormon be a part of their daily devotional study. Ezra Taft Benson became the new President of the Church in 1985 and inaugurated his prophetic ministry with addresses on the Book of Mormon's role in the Restoration. President Benson directly urged Saints to intensify their relationship with the book. Scholars heard this call in their own way and gave their attention to the Book of Mormon in a concerted effort to return to the fields that Jakeman, Nibley, and Sperry had left fallow more than a decade earlier. Rising in defense especially of the Book of Mormon's claim to antiquity, these scholars gathered around a nascent institution that would prove to be a major intellectual force in Book of Mormon studies: the Foundation for Ancient Research and Mormon Studies (FARMS), established in 1979.

FARMS's work on the Book of Mormon, with a strong emphasis on defending the Book of Mormon's origins in the ancient world, gently displaced another vision for Book of Mormon studies that had begun to emerge in the late 1970s. Gathering around the Association for Mormon Letters during those years—and certainly encouraged by the institutional support that well-trained historians were receiving from the Church—was a group of (mostly young) literary readers of the Book of Mormon. Robert K. Thomas, Bruce W. Jorgensen, Robert E. Nichols, Eugene England, Marilyn Arnold, Steven C. Walker, Richard Dilworth Rust, Steven P. Sondrup, James E. Faulconer, and Mark D. Thomas, among others, busied themselves in laying the foundation for a field of literary scholarship on the Book of Mormon. It's clear from publications by these scholars during the last years of the 1970s and the first years of the 1980s that they meant to speak as much to scholars outside the faith tradition as to scholars inside, and they had big plans. Unfortunately for literary study of the Book of Mormon, the crisis in professional Latter-day Saint history in the early 1980s that was caused in part by Mark Hofmann's forgeries, along with the increasing need to respond to criticisms of the Book of Mormon, prevented literary scholars from doing more than publish a few scattered papers on the Book of Mormon. This seems to owe especially to the fact that as the controversies of the early 1980s matured, it became in certain ways unsafe for believing scholars to speak of reading the Book of Mormon as literature. Certain critics of the Book of Mormon from within the Latter-day Saint tradition spoke of affirming the inspired nature of the Book of Mormon while rejecting its claims to ancient historicity. This dissident position came to be described as treating the Book of Mormon as sacred fiction. Believing literary readers of the Book of Mormon found themselves on difficult terrain, wishing to bring the tools used in reading fiction to reading the Book of Mormon but unsure of how to do so without being accused of disregarding the book's claims to truth. Literary study of the Book of Mormon, barely emergent, found that it had to wait for the air to clear a bit before it could proceed.

FARMS was itself a product of the late 1970s, founded initially as an independent institution to make Hugh Nibley's lesser-known essays and other apologetic resources available to interested readers. By the early 1980s, however, the organization had begun to sponsor new scholarly work on the Book of Mormon and other areas of Latter-day Saint interest, generally with an emphasis on defending the Church's claims to truth. Many scholars associated with FARMS from the beginning were eager to enlist their academic training in the service of defending the Book of Mormon against criticisms—whether those criticisms came from well-trained scholars writing for other academics or from lay Christians or pastors writing scurrilous pamphlets for popular consumption. FARMS scholars were, in short, perfectly attuned to the needs of the moment in the early 1980s. Importantly, FARMS also brought together scholars who were less interested in directly responding to specific criticisms of the Book of Mormon than in building a positive case for the book's claim to antiquity. Like Jakeman, Nibley, and Sperry, the scholars at FARMS wished to debunk the critics and make a positive case that the Book of Mormon fit well into the ancient world. By the mid-1980s, the organization had worked out a publishing deal with Church-owned Deseret Book to make its research available to a wide Latter-day Saint readership. By the end of the 1980s, FARMS scholars were publishing Hugh Nibley's collected works alongside books of their own, as well as printing an annual journal, the *Review of Books on the Book of Mormon*.

FARMS's relationship to Nibley was particularly important. John W. Welch, a law professor and FARMS's founder, unquestionably saw his work from the very beginning as continuing Nibley's. Welch made a name for himself in the late 1960s when he published an article (in *BYU Studies*) arguing that chiasmus—an ancient form of Hebrew poetry—could be found throughout the Book of Mormon. After founding FARMS, Welch began to publish through its various outlets volumes of similar work, scouring the ancient Near East for traces that paralleled aspects of the Book of Mormon. Not only did he edit many collections of essays FARMS would put into print (consistently contributing his own essays to such volumes as well), but he also published a well-received monograph in 1990 that defended against criticisms of the Book of Mormon's inclusion of a New World version of the Sermon on the Mount.[3] The most prolific of the FARMS scholars, Welch would eventually serve as an editor of all four volumes of Nibley's collected works that focus exclusively on the Book of Mormon. Well into the twenty-first century, FARMS would continue efforts to make Nibley's scholarship—including other essays on the Book of Mormon—available in print. And, naturally, FARMS scholars also honored Nibley's colleagues, Jakeman and Sperry, in Book of Mormon scholarship. John L. Sorenson's *An Ancient American Setting for the Book of Mormon*, published by FARMS and Deseret Book in 1985, was explicitly an attempt to take the kind of work that Jakeman once did and make it more academically respectable. Further, at least one issue of FARMS's later *Journal of Book of Mormon Studies* (specifically volume 4, issue 1) was dedicated to revisiting the work and legacy of Sperry's work on the Book of Mormon.

Nearly from the beginning, though, FARMS found itself in conflict with the publisher Signature Books. From the start, Signature Books, founded in 1981, included in its catalog works that raised questions about Latter-day Saint faith claims. Such works touched on the Book of Mormon with some frequency, and the battle between the two institutions came to be focused in a particular way on the Book of Mormon with Signature Book's publication in 1993 of *New Approaches to the Book of Mormon: Explorations in Critical Methodology*. The volume, edited by Brent Lee Metcalfe, is a collection of essays that, with few exceptions, explicitly aim to question traditional faith claims regarding the Book of

> "In contemporary Mormonism the main battle is not about the Bible. Although it would be wrong to conclude that Latter-day Saint scholars are uninformed or uninterested in non-Mormon biblical exegesis, what in other denominations is a battle for the Bible is in contemporary Mormonism a battle for the Book of Mormon. This battle is fought not around interpretation, but around the very nature of the Book of Mormon. Is it what it claims to be?"
>
> —Massimo Introvigne, "The Book of Mormon Wars: A Non-Mormon Perspective"

Mormon. Many of the authors of the essays pursued their task by targeting FARMS-published scholarship: Sorenson's Mesoamerican model of Book of Mormon geography, Welch's treatment of the Book of Mormon version of the Sermon on the Mount, and various FARMS scholars' work on potentially Hebraistic aspects of the Book of Mormon. FARMS responded by publishing at least nineteen direct responses to the book in four different issues of its *Review of Books on the Book of Mormon*. It also appears to have responded by increasing the intensity of its activity, since the second half of the 1990s saw an unmistakable uptick in the output of FARMS scholarship.

The conflict between FARMS and Signature Books determined the shape of Book of Mormon studies for most of the 1990s. Especially telling is that when a few of the late 1970s literary attempts to read the Book of Mormon matured in the 1990s into full books, the results were printed by the two opposing publishing outfits. Richard Dilworth Rust published *Feasting on the Word* with FARMS (and Deseret Book), while Mark Thomas published *Digging in Cumorah* with Signature Books. In the intervening years, Rust had shaped his writing so that it provided what he called a literary testimony of the Book of Mormon's truth—engaging, however gently, in the larger apologetic enterprise represented by FARMS. Thomas, for his part, professed a position of neutrality regarding faith claims, but readers pointed out right away what they felt was a secularizing and naturalizing bent in the book. Whether Thomas did or didn't succeed in achieving a position of scholarly neutrality, those at the heart of scholarly writing about the Book of Mormon largely seemed to agree that one couldn't write without taking sides on the all-consuming question of historicity. There was, as one FARMS scholar put it, no middle ground on the issue.[4]

Signature Books wasn't the only alternative to the FARMS model of Book of Mormon scholarship during the 1980s and 1990s, however. Emerging in the mid-1980s also—and unquestionably in response to Ezra Taft Benson's presidential endorsement of the Book of Mormon—was a style of devotional scholarship on the book, centered in BYU's departments of religious education. BYU's own Religious Studies Center began hosting an annual Book of Mormon Symposium on campus in 1985 and then began publishing the proceedings in 1988. Scholars writing for this venue developed what they—in honor of their chief model, the then recently deceased Apostle Bruce R. McConkie—labeled *doctrinal* study of the Book of Mormon. Explicitly devotional and believing but nonetheless reflecting training and scholarly interest, the essays that made up this eventually nine-volume series represent a distinct approach to the text. They took the Book of Mormon largely as an occasion for theological and pastoral reflection. This unique style of scholarship reached a peak in the early 1990s when Bookcraft published a four-volume *Doctrinal Commentary on the Book of Mormon*, penned by its major representatives: Joseph Fielding McConkie, Robert L. Millet, and Brent L. Top.

Generally speaking, doctrinal scholarship didn't conflict with the historically minded scholarship produced by FARMS. When FARMS launched a second journal in 1992, the *Journal of Book of Mormon Studies*, the new editor invited doctrinal scholar Robert Millet to serve as a member of the editorial board, and Millet contributed an article to the journal in its second year. And Stephen E. Robinson, Millet's colleague, had already reviewed Dan Vogel's *The Word of God* in 1991 for FARMS. There were, however, times when the doctrinal orientation of BYU's religious educators during the 1980s and 1990s conflicted with the historical orientation of FARMS's publications. A good example occurred in 1989 when FARMS scholar Louis Midgley published in FARMS's *Review of*

Books on the Book of Mormon a deeply critical review of the first volumes of McConkie and Millet's *Doctrinal Commentary*. Generally, however, both approaches were welcome at BYU, which became unmistakably clear when, in 1997, FARMS received an invitation to become a formal part of the university. FARMS had been working informally in and around BYU's campus almost since its founding. It now moved on campus officially and thus received a stamp of approval for its work.

The same year of 1997 also saw FARMS receive a rather unofficial but no less real gesture of encouragement. That year, evangelical scholars Carl Mosser and Paul Owen presented a joint paper at a conference of their colleagues arguing that FARMS scholars were winning the academic war for the Book of Mormon. Of course, Mosser and Owen presented (and later published) their paper specifically to spur a stronger and better-informed critique of the Book of Mormon (and of various Latter-day Saint faith claims). But this admission of FARMS's intellectual successes from outside, despite continuing struggles against Book of Mormon critics from within the Latter-day Saint tradition, indicated to many that FARMS had by the end of the twentieth century effectively established the intellectual credibility of the Book of Mormon as an ancient text. It's no coincidence, it seems, that the last years of the 1990s were FARMS's most productive years. These particular years saw into print a truly remarkable series of books on the Book of Mormon: *Isaiah in the Book of Mormon*, *King Benjamin's Speech*, *Book of Mormon Authorship Revisited*, and (the aforementioned) *Feasting on the Word*, among others. Perhaps especially impressive was the 1996 publication of *A Comprehensive Annotated Book of Mormon Bibliography*—with more than six hundred pages of bibliographic entries on the whole history of published writing about the Book of Mormon. As the twentieth century wound to a close, it seemed that the future of Book of Mormon studies couldn't be brighter and that FARMS would lead the way into the new millennium.

Through the whole of its twentieth-century sojourn, from the mid-1940s to the late 1990s, Book of Mormon studies found its center of

> The twentieth-century question: Is the Book of Mormon the ancient text it claims to be?

gravity in one question: Is the Book of Mormon the ancient text it claims to be? All three founders of the scholarly discipline—Sidney Sperry, M. Wells Jakeman, and Hugh Nibley—took this as their central question, even if they approached the task of answering it differently. The question wasn't one they invented either; it was a question that Fawn Brodie, like others before her, effectively presented to them, since she'd attempted to bring together evidence that the Book of Mormon was a nineteenth-century product of Joseph Smith's peculiar religious genius. When it felt like Sperry, Jakeman, and Nibley had done the necessary work to demonstrate that one could endorse the Book of Mormon's antiquity while respectably holding one's scholarly head up, academic work on the Book of Mormon slowed and nearly disappeared. It was only once historians and critics raised the old Brodie-like questions again in the early 1980s that Book of Mormon studies rematerialized as a recognizable intellectual force. But what emerged in the 1980s was a more complex field of research. FARMS scholars occupied the center of the field, claiming the legacies of Jakeman, Nibley, and Sperry. Critical scholars vied directly with FARMS scholars for control of the field, while devotional and doctrinal readers found places for themselves in and around the central conflict. Even literary readers hovered about the borders of the field, waiting for opportunities to say something about the Book of Mormon. In all this, however, the very first questions asked by Book of Mormon scholars at mid-century remained the most frequently asked and answered ones.

In the first years of the twenty-first century, a brilliant and charged analysis of all these developments appeared—largely without warning. In 2002, Oxford University Press published Terryl L. Givens's *By the Hand of Mormon: The American Scripture That Launched a New World Religion*. The book presented itself as a reception history—that is, as a study of how people of various persuasions have tried, over nearly two centuries, to make sense of the Book of Mormon. Because it isn't itself a direct endorsement of the Book of Mormon or its claims, and because it's a sophisticated and deeply subtle work of scholarship, *By the Hand of Mormon* could be issued by a publisher well outside the debates that so charged the atmosphere of the 1980s and 1990s. At the same time, one of the major subjects covered in *By the Hand of Mormon* is precisely

Book of Mormon Studies

those very debates of the 1980s and 1990s. Givens took those disputes—and FARMS's successes in those disputes—as confirmations of his overarching thesis. The central argument in *By the Hand of Mormon* is that the Book of Mormon's central theological contribution lies not in its actual content or message but rather in the way the Book of Mormon points beyond the Bible to new revelation. It's the very idea of ongoing revelation, and specifically what Givens called "dialogic revelation," that makes the Latter-day Saint faith a radical one.[5]

> **DEFINITION**
>
> **Dialogic revelation:** Revelation that comes to human beings in actual words; direct communication from God.

For Givens in *By the Hand of Mormon*, then, the wrangling over historicity throughout the twentieth century is evidence of his point that the Book of Mormon has principally embodied new revelation. The struggle had never been about the *meaning* of the Book of Mormon but only about its *truth* and derivatively about Joseph Smith's divine calling. Further, Givens took the fact that FARMS had made a seriously convincing case for Book of Mormon historicity—serious enough to wring a confession of something like temporary defeat from evangelical opponents—to mean that the Book of Mormon debates could be, in a certain fashion, set aside. FARMS had essentially won the war, and so the real question had to become something else now, something built on the solid foundation of the Book of Mormon's validity: What did Joseph Smith, the Prophet whose calling had been confirmed through the exoneration of the book he set before the world, actually have to say in his own teachings? What was Joseph Smith's theological vision after and beyond the Book of Mormon? Although Givens would occasionally write in subsequent years about the Book of Mormon again, his developing project would confirm most of the time that he felt that the real contribution of the Restoration to the world lay elsewhere than in the Book of Mormon.

Givens's watershed book was thus a deeply complex phenomenon. It announced to the larger scholarly world that the Book of Mormon was academically respectable—that FARMS scholars,

By the Hand of Mormon

building on the work of their predecessors, had done their work responsibly and well. *By the Hand of Mormon*, in other words, effectively gave the FARMS scholars leave to take at least a temporary vacation from their burnout pace. They could breathe a little easier than they had for a long time. But Givens's book also presented the same larger scholarly world with a muddled message about the Book of Mormon. The upshot of Givens's argument was that the Book of Mormon was a divine arrow pointing to the prophetic gifts of Joseph Smith, who should be the real subject of study. But because Givens made that argument by giving three hundred pages of a scholarly publication to the study of the Book of Mormon, he also made clear that there was real potential for nonpartisan scholarly writing about the Book of Mormon. Thus, ironically, it was less the actual content of Givens's argument than what *By the Hand of Mormon* enacted that would prove significant for Book of Mormon studies. Givens showed that there was space—as literary scholars in the late 1970s had surmised—for a version of Book of Mormon scholarship that might be uninterested in debating questions of historicity.

> **STYLES OF WRITING ABOUT THE BOOK OF MORMON**
>
> • *Devotional* (confessional) writing
> • *Apologetic* (defensive) argument
> • *Neutral* (secular) analysis

There was in fact a literary reader of the Book of Mormon fully ready to take advantage of such a situation, simply waiting for the moment Givens created. Already in 2000, Grant Hardy had written a review of Mark Thomas's *Digging in Cumorah* in the *FARMS Review of Books* (a retitled version of the *Review of Books on the Book of Mormon*), announcing that, although he didn't think Thomas had quite acquired the neutral voice he'd have liked, he did think Thomas had the right idea. In 2003, only a year after *By the Hand of Mormon* appeared, Hardy published with the University of Illinois Press his *Reader's Edition* of the Book of Mormon, an edition of the volume of scripture deliberately oriented to the literarily inclined reader (and, significantly, published by an academic press outside Utah). A few years later, in 2010, his *Understanding the Book of Mormon: A Reader's Guide*, published by Oxford University Press, would appear and receive universal acclaim. Hardy's

Book of Mormon Studies

TIMELINE OF BOOK OF MORMON RESEARCH

Year(s)	Name(s)	Event(s)
1879	Orson Pratt	Publication of the first study-oriented edition of the Book of Mormon
1890–1930	George Reynolds, B. H. Roberts, Janne M. Sjödahl	Appearance of early resources for studying the Book of Mormon (such as dictionaries and concordances), as well as preliminary studies of the text itself
1920	James E. Talmage	Publication of a new study-oriented edition of the Book of Mormon
1945	Fawn M. Brodie	Publication of *No Man Knows My History*, a popular biography of Joseph Smith that called Book of Mormon origins into question
1940–1970	Sidney B. Sperry, Hugh W. Nibley, M. Wells Jakeman	The rise of the first university-trained scholars to work on the Book of Mormon, who were focused especially on defending the book's claim to be an ancient work
1965–1985	New Mormon history	A movement aiming at professionalization for the study of Latter-day Saint history, eventually raising questions about the Book of Mormon's historical origins
1976–1979	Association for Mormon Letters (AML), Foundation for Ancient Research and Mormon Studies (FARMS)	The founding of new organizations sponsoring scholarship on the Book of Mormon, with AML promoting literary study of the scripture and FARMS promoting Nibley-like historical study of the scripture
1980–1985	Mark Hofmann, Signature Books, countercultism	Direct and indirect cultural pressures bearing on the Book of Mormon's claims to divinity and ancient origins
1981–1986	Ezra Taft Benson	A new edition of the Book of Mormon, a new subtitle for the book ("Another Testament of Jesus Christ"), and a series of sermons promoting the centrality of the Book of Mormon to Latter-day Saint devotion
1981–2000	FARMS, Signature Books, Brigham Young University Religious Education	The so-called Book of Mormon culture wars, massive acceleration of FARMS publications (including journals, with the *Review of Books on the Book of Mormon* first published in 1989 and the *Journal of Book of Mormon Studies* in 1992), and the emergence of a doctrinal school of Book of Mormon research (at BYU)

TIMELINE OF BOOK OF MORMON RESEARCH

Year(s)	Name(s)	Event(s)
1997	FARMS	Brigham Young University's invitation to FARMS to become a formal and sponsored part of the campus community
2002	Terryl Givens	Publication of *By the Hand of Mormon*, modeling a new approach to Book of Mormon studies while FARMS slows down
2002–2022	Neal A. Maxwell Institute for Religious Scholarship, Grant Hardy, Latter-day Saint Theology Seminar	New labors and institutions promoting a wider variety of scholarly approaches to the Book of Mormon (especially literary and theological approaches), with the Maxwell Institute replacing FARMS at BYU in 2006

readings and labors were emphatically literary (they were specifically narratological—that is, attuned to how storytellers in the Book of Mormon go about telling their stories). And he was explicit that his aim was to leave debates over the historicity of the Book of Mormon out of his reading, hoping to construct an approach to and interpretation of the book that might be read with appreciation by outsiders to the faith as much as by insiders.

Hardy's appearance on the scene in the wake of Givens's *By the Hand of Mormon* coincided with a noticeable slowdown in FARMS's production schedule. The first few years of the twenty-first century saw FARMS symposia and publications reduced to a trickle. The *Journal of Book of Mormon Studies* had changed its format in 1998, but then it changed its title in 2008 to the *Journal of the Book of Mormon and Other Restoration Scripture*—broadening its scope even as the size of the journal shrank. Annual symposia slowed considerably in the first years of the new century, with only one major collection of essays on the Book of Mormon appearing in 2004 (*Glimpses of Lehi's Jerusalem*). *Echoes and Evidences of the Book of Mormon*, an encyclopedic summary of past FARMS research, appeared in 2002, suggesting that the work had largely been done and could now be anthologized and simply made more accessible. The *Review of Books on the Book of Mormon* became the *FARMS Review of Books* in 1996 and then the *FARMS Review* in 2003, broadening its scope several times over as it seemed there was less to say about the Book of Mormon. The field that FARMS had plowed for Book of Mormon scholarship was increasingly appearing to lie fallow.

It was into this fallow field that literary readers like Hardy came—but also, very soon after, theological readers such as Adam Miller and his Latter-day Saint Theology Seminar (initially the Mormon Theology Seminar). It was over the course of the two decades following the publication of *By the Hand of Mormon* that an explosion of interest in the Book of Mormon from the larger academic establishment occurred. By the beginning of the 2020s, articles and book chapters and whole monographs on the Book of Mormon were appearing throughout the academy, and intense interest in Book of Mormon scholarship had begun to take hold anew—and with a wider variety of approaches on display—among believing scholars. It's time now, then, to explain the basic contours of the field that's taken shape in the twenty-first century.

NOTES

1. For the traditional assessment of Latter-day Saints' reception of the Book of Mormon, see especially Philip L. Barlow, *Mormons and the Bible: The Place of the Latter-day Saints in American Religion* (New York: Oxford University Press, 1991), 11–42; Grant Underwood, "Book of Mormon Usage in Early LDS Theology," *Dialogue: A Journal of Mormon Thought* 17, no. 3 (Autumn 1984): 35–74; Noel B. Reynolds, "The Coming Forth of the Book of Mormon in the Twentieth Century," *BYU Studies* 38, no. 2 (1999): 6–47; and Terryl L. Givens, *By the Hand of Mormon: The American Scripture That Launched a World Religion* (New York: Oxford University Press, 2002), 62–88. For the most important recent work that clarifies early reception, see Janiece Johnson, "Becoming a People of the Books: Toward an Understanding of Early Mormon Converts and the New Word of the Lord," *Journal of Book of Mormon Studies* 27 (2018): 1–43.
2. See, naturally, Sidney B. Sperry, *The Problems of the Book of Mormon* (Salt Lake City: Bookcraft, 1964).
3. See John W. Welch, *The Sermon at the Temple and the Sermon on the Mount* (Provo, UT: FARMS; Salt Lake City, UT: Deseret Book, 1990).
4. See Louis Midgley, "No Middle Ground: The Debate over the Authenticity of the Book of Mormon," in *Historicity and the Latter-day Saint Scriptures*, ed. Paul Y. Hoskisson (Provo, UT: Religious Studies Center, Brigham Young University, 2001), 149–70.
5. See Givens, *By the Hand of Mormon*, 209–39.

| CHAPTER 2 |

The Field

As we've indicated, Book of Mormon studies has flourished in the first decades of the twenty-first century. In fact, scholars have broken new ground on so many topics—and have done their groundbreaking work in such a variety of venues—that it can be hard to get a sense for the field as a whole. It's time, then, to survey that field. In doing so, we hope to provide readers with a map that's clear enough to guide them wherever they want to go. The following survey divides the field into its seven major areas of ongoing research—the seven subdisciplines of Book of Mormon studies. For each, we provide a basic sketch of its history, an outline of major developments in the past two decades, and a summary of its current state and promise for the future. Full bibliographic information for any works and authors mentioned, as well as further information about publishing outfits and research institutions, can be found in the appendix.

TEXTUAL PRODUCTION

A first major area of research—as old as the discipline of Book of Mormon studies but greatly enhanced by the work of many historians in recent years—focuses on what's often called the "coming forth" of the Book of Mormon. While events surrounding the Book of Mormon's dictation and publication drew attention from the beginning, scholarly conversation on the topic really began after Fawn M. Brodie's 1945 work *No Man Knows My History: The Life of Joseph Smith*. Brodie argued that Joseph Smith, impressed by Native American mounds in western New York, set out to explain how the peaceful and culturally advanced mound-builder civilization was destroyed by its more violent and primitive neighbors. According to Brodie, the young Joseph initially intended to write a secular and explicitly fictional account—hoping only to make money for his impoverished family—but then decided for complicated reasons to transform the project into something religious and allegedly nonfictional. Brodie's work was to that point the most sophisticated attack on the origins of the Book of Mormon. For Brodie, the Book of Mormon wasn't sacred text but frontier mythology. When Hugh W. Nibley published a fierce rebuttal to Brodie's work, humorously entitled *No, Ma'am, That's Not History*, and then when scholars like Richard Lloyd Anderson contested much of Brodie's primary evidence, this first category of research—the textual production of the Book of Mormon—was effectively born. Its aim is simply to reconstruct as responsibly as possible the circumstances surrounding the translation and publication of the Book of Mormon.

> **SUBDISCIPLINES IN BOOK OF MORMON STUDIES**
>
> · Textual production
> · Historical origins
> · Literary criticism
> · Intertextuality
> · Theological interpretation
> · Reception history
> · Ideology critique

After his initial response to Brodie, Nibley waited until the 1960s to reflect at length on the historical circumstances of the Book of Mormon's coming forth. His work coincided with the rise of the "new Mormon history" movement that soon furnished scholars with more specialized training and serious time for archival and library research on the subject. By the 1980s, important and enduring research on the matter began to appear. Two books in particular appeared that would guide and shape further research: Richard L. Bushman's *Joseph Smith and the Beginnings of Mormonism* and D. Michael Quinn's *Early Mormonism and the Magic World View*. The latter, drawing on Joseph Smith's youthful connections to folk magic, painted a picture in which the Book of Mormon was translated in the midst of a deeply enchanted culture on the margins of polite society. A decade later, John L. Brooke's *The Refiner's Fire* would develop this approach to Book of Mormon origins even further. Bushman's study, however, foreshadowing what he'd do twenty years later in *Joseph Smith: Rough Stone Rolling*, presented a more measured account of things. Bushman placed the young Prophet in a historically and socially complex New England, from which he emerged with a clear sense of mission and purpose—and with a sacred book in hand.

In the twenty-first century, historians have generally followed the tradition of Bushman's book. They've done so, though, with the added benefit of the systematic labors of the Joseph Smith Papers Project. Michael Hubbard MacKay and Gerrit J. Dirkmaat brought such research to a remarkable first fruition in what is now the standard treatment of the coming forth of the Book of Mormon: *From Darkness unto Light*, published in 2015. (A follow-up that focused just on the use of seer stones was published the next year, written by MacKay and Nicholas J. Frederick.) MacKay and Dirkmaat's book breaks much new ground; for example, it weaves a much more complex story about Martin Harris's famous trip to visit scholars in New York City. This kind of work, though, has in many ways only begun. Recent studies—such as articles by Robin Scott Jensen and Angela Erdmann, for instance—show that much remains to be learned from close historical investigation of events surrounding the printing of the first edition of the Book of Mormon. Especially novel in this regard is Don Bradley's recent book *The Lost 116 Pages: Reconstructing the Book of Mormon's Missing Stories*—a much-anticipated study of historical sources surrounding the famed lost manuscript. Consensus about the production of the

From Darkness unto Light

Book of Mormon has been reached on many points, but the ground has been cleared for more specialized research. And it's likely that much of that more specialized research will have major and unanticipated interpretive and historical implications.

A subject of particular importance for students of the Book of Mormon's coming forth—one that has not settled into consensus—is the mechanics of the translation process. How did the original language on the gold plates become the English text of the Book of Mormon? Joseph Smith was hesitant to speak about this issue, as authors often note, but believers and critics have long expressed interest in it. Eyewitnesses to the text's dictation were less reticent than Joseph, providing descriptions in various interviews in the nineteenth century. Serious discussion of these primary sources, however, began only with B. H. Roberts in the twentieth century. Roberts was the first to seriously broach the practical difficulties posed by the Book of Mormon translation, both in reconciling witness statements with each other and in making sense of the English text of the Book of Mormon itself. Roberts pushed back against the lay notion that the Prophet simply dictated the text he saw in the Nephite interpreters, arguing for a more complex process. According to Roberts, Joseph divinely received facts and ideas and then worked to express these in his own language. This would explain apparent deficiencies in the Book of Mormon text, such as errors in spelling and grammar. Roberts further argued that when the Prophet came to sections of the Nephite record with a significant parallel in the King James Bible (like the so-called Isaiah chapters), he used a copy of the Bible as the basis for the English text.

Roberts's contemporaries and immediate successors in the Latter-day Saint intellectual community largely agreed with him, although some (such as Elder John A. Widtsoe and BYU professor Sidney B. Sperry) worked to soften aspects of Roberts's account. Their concerns grew out of increasing awareness that, in discussing the translation of the Book of Mormon, the historicity of the text might be at stake. Cavalier suggestions that Joseph Smith provided the language of the Book of Mormon raised questions about whether the book revealed more about its ancient authors or about Joseph Smith. Discussions of the actual mechanics of the translation process thus soon took a back seat

> "All the circumstances connected with the work of translation clearly prove that it caused the Prophet the utmost exertion, mental and spiritual, of which he was capable, and while he obtained the facts and ideas from the Nephite characters, he was left to express those ideas in such language as he was master of."
>
> —B. H. Roberts, "Elder Roberts's Reply to Criticism on the Book of Mormon," *Salt Lake Tribune*, November 29, 1903

---

to the quest to prove historical authenticity. Leading the charge in this direction was Nibley in his 1960s treatments of the coming forth of the Book of Mormon. Nibley argued that questions about seer stones and the like were ultimately distracting and that just trusting that Joseph's translations were dependent on revelation was enough.

Nibley's work was highly influential, with scholars at the Foundation for Ancient Research and Mormon Studies (FARMS) in the 1980s and 1990s often assuming that Joseph Smith wasn't a source for the Book of Mormon text. Pointing to poetic structures and Hebrew idioms that seem to have survived the process of translation into the English text of the Book of Mormon, FARMS scholars also downplayed the mechanics of translation. Meanwhile, however, historians intrigued by increased clarity about the Prophet's youthful folk-magic associations developed a relative scholarly consensus about the mechanics of translation and the use of seer stones—exemplified in Richard Van Wagoner and Steve Walker's "Joseph Smith: 'The Gift of Seeing.'" Late in the 1980s, however, an oft-cited paper by Blake Ostler appeared in *Dialogue: A Journal of Mormon Thought*, arguing that the English text of the Book of Mormon represents a considerable expansion of an ancient text. For Ostler, in some ways revitalizing the conversation among Roberts, Widtsoe, and Sperry, the Prophet had access to a real Nephite record but also had the freedom to cast it in his own language, even in certain ways misrepresenting the original sources. Ostler's position was received at the time as somewhat extreme, but it became relatively common among scholars by the early twenty-first century—one of several ways of defending the antiquity of the Book of Mormon without needing to explain away every alleged trace of nineteenth-century influence in the English text of the book.

During the first decade of the twenty-first century, then, the conversation on Book of Mormon translation largely halted between two positions. The first was the one inherited from FARMS and has been most strongly represented by Royal Skousen (in various publications), who has argued that the Book of Mormon text was transmitted directly to Joseph Smith (largely) without the latter's influence—that is, with "tight control." Skousen developed the traditional FARMS position beyond that of the 1980s and 1990s, however, arguing (alongside his colleague Stanford Carmack) that the English text of the Book of Mormon belongs to the sixteenth rather than the nineteenth century. The second position was best represented by Brant A. Gardner (in *The Gift and Power*). Gardner has overtly defended the antiquity and Mesoamerican setting of the Book of Mormon. At the same time, he argues that Joseph Smith recast the ancient book in at least a gently nineteenth-century guise. Arguing thus for a model of "loose control" over the translation process, Gardner updated and clarified Ostler's earlier work.

By the end of the 2010s, however, it was clear that numerous authors had grown dissatisfied with the two standard positions on Book of Mormon translation. In part, this is because both approaches are of interest only to believing scholars, leaving out increasingly interested scholars working from outside the faith tradition. Some believers, however, have also felt constrained by these two standard positions. The year 2020 saw the publication of a major book-length study of the idea of translation in Joseph Smith's career (Samuel Morris Brown's *Joseph Smith's Translation*), as well as a large collection of essays (*Producing Ancient Scripture*) on the same subject with strikingly inventive articles on the Book of Mormon's translation by authors like Samuel Brown, Richard Bushman, Grant Hardy, Jared Hickman, and others. All this very recent work points in rather different directions, suggesting that the conversation about Book of Mormon translation is still ongoing.

HISTORICAL ORIGINS

A second area of ongoing Book of Mormon research concerns the historical circumstances of the Book of Mormon's original creation (not just its translation or dictation). Some scholars seek these origins in the ancient world (often motivated by faith in the book's claims about itself), while others seek them in the modern world (often motivated by skepticism about the book's claims). Like questions about the coming forth of the Book of Mormon, questions about historical origins arose as early as when the book came into print. Here again, though, it's arguably only with Fawn Brodie and Hugh Nibley, positioned at opposite extremes, that the issue came into its own as an area of scholarly research. Before them, those who wrote on the subject ventured opinions and defended them with scattershot data rather than sifting carefully through historical sources to build an intellectually defensible case. In *No Man Knows My History*, as already noted, Brodie developed a theory of how the Book of Mormon came into being. In direct response to Brodie, Nibley began in the late 1940s—and continued into the mid-1960s—to gather extensive data that might situate the Book of Mormon squarely in the ancient world. Proficient in numerous languages and well trained in a scholarly field that had been around for centuries, Nibley brought the wealth of classical learning to studying Book of Mormon origins. In three books that all began as Church publications in one way or another, Nibley argued that the best way to defend Book of Mormon historicity was to examine its rootedness in an Old World setting rather than to search for archaeological traces of the book in the New World.

A hundred years of amateur and hobbyist archaeological speculation about the Book of Mormon's ancient historical setting preceded Nibley's interventions. For that reason, Nibley took aim as much against such speculation as against critics of Book of Mormon historicity. During the very years of Nibley's entry into Book of Mormon studies, though, amateur Book of Mormon archaeology began to give way to Book of Mormon archaeology undertaken by trained specialists —most crucially at first, M. Wells Jakeman. Despite his training, Jakeman's work was often tendentious and problematic, and Nibley criticized it both privately and publicly during the 1950s. Both Nibley and Jakeman eventually produced followers, however, who pushed forward their respective efforts at setting the Book of Mormon in the ancient world. The two intellectuals' heirs apparent—John W. Welch for Nibley and John L. Sorenson for Jakeman—agreed with each other much more readily than their predecessors. And so the search for Book of Mormon origins in the ancient Near East and in the ancient Americas became a kind of unified program in the 1980s, undertaken amicably by the scholars gathered about FARMS. Sorenson's 1985 *An Ancient American Setting for the Book of Mormon* set Jakeman's archaeological work on better footing, while Welch's enormous literary output on the Book of Mormon (including his often selfless work of editing others' scholarship for publication) continued in the vein Nibley had carved out. Welch also oversaw the editing and republication of Nibley's writings on the Book of Mormon in four volumes of Nibley's *Collected Works* in the late 1980s.

The 1980s also witnessed the rise of Brodie's direct heirs, mostly gathered around Signature Books. Building on professionalized Latter-day Saint history, these scholars—with Dan Vogel at their head—worked to gather evidence that supported nineteenth-century origins for the Book of Mormon. Especially in *Indian Origins and the Book of Mormon* (but also later in *Joseph Smith: The Making of a Prophet*), Vogel worked to develop and substantiate Brodie's relatively brief treatment of the Book of Mormon. He also gathered work by other scholars into a 1990 collection of essays, *The Word of God: Essays on Mormon Scripture*, that drew heavy fire from Stephen E. Robinson in the FARMS-published *Review of Books on the Book of Mormon*. A volley followed. Vogel and his colleagues responded with a direct assault on FARMS's scholarship in essays gathered under the title *New Approaches to the Book of Mormon*, edited by Brent Lee Metcalfe and published in 1993. Many essays in the volume examined FARMS scholars' historical methods—the methods of those defending the Book of Mormon's ancient Near Eastern roots *and* of those defending its ancient American setting. This collection of essays in turn drew a spirited response and cemented a controversy between Brodie's and Nibley's heirs that continued to the end of the decade and beyond.

By the end of the 1990s, FARMS was producing historically oriented scholarship more prolifically than ever, and Signature Books continued to respond with naturalizing responses. But as the twentieth century gave way to the twenty-first—and especially with the appearance of Terryl L. Givens's *By the Hand of Mormon: The American Scripture That Launched a New World Religion*—the intensity of the conflict lessened. As the first decade of the twenty-first century wore on, the *FARMS Review* (once titled the *Review of Books on the Book of Mormon*) and the *Journal of the Book of Mormon and Other Restoration Scripture* (once titled the *Journal of Book of Mormon Studies*) broadened their focuses and largely left the Book of Mormon behind. And with a professional discipline of "Mormon studies" taking root after Givens's book—and especially after Richard Bushman's 2005 *Joseph Smith: Rough Stone Rolling*—Brodie's heirs grew quieter as well. The larger FARMS project, in its ancient Near Eastern and ancient American dimensions, found itself funneled into the remarkable six-volume Book of Mormon commentary *Second Witness*, hosted online for a time and then published by Greg Kofford Books. Written single-handedly by Brant Gardner, this commentary summed up and read critically the Old World research of 1980s and 1990s FARMS scholars while it also inherited and extended the New World research produced by Sorenson and others at FARMS.

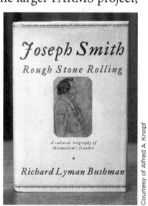

Joseph Smith: Rough Stone Rolling

Since Gardner's commentary (and his follow-up volume, *Traditions of the Fathers: The Book of Mormon as History*), historical research on the Book of Mormon has slowed somewhat—both defensive and critical. An explosion of popular interest in the Latter-day Saint tradition during the years surrounding Mitt Romney's 2012 presidential campaign boosted already-growing scholarly interest. And in that climate, there was more interest than ever before in nonpartisan discussions of aspects of the Latter-day Saint faith, the Book of Mormon included. Talk of "bracketing" the question of the Book of Mormon's historical origins to study the text in its own right has become common—and has been fundamental to the early twenty-first century's most important book on the Book of Mormon, Grant Hardy's 2010 *Understanding the Book of Mormon*. As publications in the *Mormon Interpreter* (later renamed *Interpreter: A Journal of Latter-day Saint Faith and Scholarship*) show, there nonetheless remains much work to do on the historical origins of the Book of Mormon—especially to tame the zeal of amateur archaeologists who claim more than the evidence allows. Some of the best work of this sort is being done by members of BYU's Book of Mormon Academy: Kerry Hull and Mark Alan Wright on the Book of Mormon ancient American setting and Daniel L. Belnap and Avram R. Shannon on the book's ancient Near Eastern roots.

LITERARY CRITICISM

A third and growing area of research in Book of Mormon studies focuses on literary criticism. Whereas Hugh Nibley's work could draw on centuries of research into the ancient Near East, bringing the Book of Mormon into contact with an old and established discipline, literary readers of the Book of Mormon have taken their cue from a much newer style of scholarship. Literary criticism on the Bible began to appear in earnest only in the middle of the twentieth century, given a name and an impetus in many ways by Northrop Frye's 1957 *Anatomy of Criticism*. The first serious literary work on the Book of Mormon actually appeared slightly earlier, beginning with Sidney Sperry's *Our Book of Mormon* in 1947. Sperry himself was skeptical about the literary value of the Book of Mormon, and his literary work on the book was more limited than that of the school of biblical literary criticism that would soon appear. While Sperry therefore limited himself to identifying literary genres in the Book of Mormon, he's often looked back to as having paved the way for a new approach to the Book of Mormon.

As literary approaches to the Bible grew in popularity during the 1970s, literary readers of the Book of Mormon began to appear as well. This included scholars, such as John W. Welch and Noel B. Reynolds, who, like Sperry before them, had training in ancient languages. They scoured the text, looking for Hebrew poetic forms. But by the late 1970s, something new was stirring. While Welch and Reynolds fused their literary interests with an aim to establish the ancient historicity of the text, other scholars began to write with more purely literary inter-

> **APPROACHES TO THE HISTORICAL ORIGINS OF THE BOOK OF MORMON**
>
> | Theory/Approach | Major Figures/Movements |
> |---|---|
> | The Book of Mormon is an ancient document, as will be demonstrated through historical, anthropological, linguistic, and archaeological study of the ancient Americas. | M. Wells Jakeman and John Sorenson in the twentieth century; Brant Gardner, Mark Wright, and Kerry Hull in the early twenty-first century (focused principally on Mesoamerica); various figures promoting other geographical locations |
> | The Book of Mormon is an ancient document, as will be demonstrated through comparative study of the text and ancient Near Eastern documents and sources. | Hugh Nibley and the Foundation for Ancient Research and Mormon Studies in the twentieth century; scholars publishing in the *Interpreter* in the twenty-first century |
> | The Book of Mormon is a modern document and so should be studied as a product of nineteenth-century culture and influences. | Fawn Brodie, various historians, and those gathered around Signature Books in the twentieth century; various historians in the twenty-first century |

ests. Studies by George S. Tate, Steven P. Sondrup, Bruce W. Jorgensen, Richard Dilworth Rust, and Mark D. Thomas, among others, appeared in the last years of the 1970s and first years of the 1980s. Initially these scholars gathered about a new organization with a variety of literary interests, the Association for Mormon Letters. As their work began to draw wider attention, however, they contributed important essays on the Book of Mormon to a 1981 volume published by BYU's Religious Studies Center under the title *Literature of Belief*. Several contributors were speaking at the time of grand projects that would bring the Book of Mormon's literary contributions into focus.

Most literary study of scripture in the 1970s and 1980s emphasized study of the text alone—its structure, message, and use of literary devices—rather than its social or historical background. Dominant methods included rhetorical analysis (focused on explaining the author's

> **AN EXAMPLE OF HEBREW POETIC FORM: CHIASMUS**
>
> And now it shall come to pass, that whosoever shall not take upon him *the name of Christ*
>   must be *called* by some other name;
>   therefore, he findeth himself on the *left hand of God*.
>   And I would that ye should *remember* also, that this is the name that I said I should give unto you
>   that should never be *blotted out*,
>   except it be through *transgression*;
>   therefore, take heed that ye do not *transgress*,
>   that the name be not *blotted out* of your hearts.
>   I say unto you, I would that ye should *remember* to retain the name written always in your hearts,
>   that ye are not found on the *left hand of God*,
>   but that ye hear and know the voice by which ye shall be *called*, and also,
> the *name* by which he shall call you.
>
>   (Mosiah 5:10–12)

intentions through investigation of poetic devices, structure, and word choice), formal analysis (focused on scripture's artful use of language, repetition, dialogue, allusion, and ambiguity to generate meaning), and narrative criticism (focused on analyzing constitutive features of storytelling, such as plot, setting, characters, point of view, the narrator, the implied author, and the implied reader). As the 1980s wore on, however, the roads traveled by literary criticism in biblical studies and literary criticism in Book of Mormon studies diverged. In biblical studies, literary criticism grew still more popular, securing its position as a compelling alternative to tired debates over traditional historical methods. In Book of Mormon studies, however, historical research made an important resurgence, as we have seen. Historical work in fact became important enough in the 1980s and then the 1990s to cause the near-total exclusion of literary criticism that didn't immediately align itself with a historical program of one sort or another. Especially after an essay in Brent Metcalfe's *New Approaches to the Book of Mormon* endorsed treating the Book of Mormon as (what was sloganized at the time as) "sacred fiction," it became particularly fraught to engage in Book of Mormon literary criticism.

Three books heralded a return of literary criticism to Book of Mormon studies in the late 1990s: Marilyn Arnold's *Sweet Is the Word: Reflections on the Book of Mormon—Its Narrative, Teachings, and People*; Richard Dilworth Rust's *Feasting on the Word: The Literary Testimony of the Book of Mormon*; and Mark D. Thomas's *Digging in Cumorah: Reclaiming Book of Mormon Narratives*. All three authors offered straightforward literary analyses of the Book of Mormon that resumed the work done in the late 1970s and early 1980s, devoting attention to the artful use of language, imagery, symbolism, syntax, narrative viewpoint, compositional unities, poetic devices, literary genres, characterization, plot, and so on. Such literary work also found advocates like Edgar Snow, James E. Faulconer, and especially Alan Goff, who argued that literary insights and literary criticism's underlying theoretical framework might be useful to defenders of Book of Mormon history. Since that time, literary interpretations have become an increasingly prolific and significant part of Book of Mormon studies.

> **DEFINITION**
>
> Literary criticism:
> A type of criticism that, when applied to scripture, involves analysis of how a text organizes the stories and ideas it presents to the reader, especially focusing on the way form gives shape to content.

For a breakthrough literary study of the Book of Mormon, though—one that also brought the literary value of the Book of Mormon to the attention of outsiders—one had to wait until the twenty-first century. This came in the form of Grant Hardy's 2010 study published by Oxford University Press, *Understanding the Book of Mormon*. Hardy had already written in 2000 an appreciation of literary work in the *FARMS Review* and published in 2003 a *Reader's Edition* of the Book of Mormon. He made good on the implicit promises of these premonitory works in *Understanding the Book of Mormon*. By explicitly bracketing questions of historicity and authorship and focusing instead on the form and sophistication of the text via its narrators, Hardy modeled an approach meant to allow believers and nonbelievers alike to engage productively with the text. Using the major narrators of the Book of

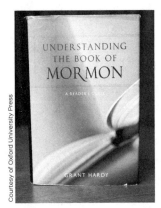

Understanding the Book of Mormon

Mormon to organize his discussion, Hardy illustrated their representative literary techniques (such as repetition, chiasmus, intertextuality, and flashbacks). He also, though, revealed underlying organizational structures in the text that are often obscure to those approaching the text with strictly doctrinal or historical concerns. When brought to the surface, such organizational structures make the text more accessible, particularly for those less familiar with it. Hardy combines a macroscopic view of the text with insightful microscopic readings of shorter passages, making his work seminal for anyone wishing to engage with the Book of Mormon as literature.

It quickly became apparent that Hardy's book marked a watershed moment. Literary readers of the Book of Mormon began to appear afterward in surprising numbers. Articles soon started to appear in the *Journal of Book of Mormon Studies*—exemplarily, Kylie Turley's "Alma's Hell: Repentance, Consequence, and the Lake of Fire and Brimstone"; Samuel Mitchell's "'Caught with Guile': Tricksters in the Book of Mormon"; and Michael Austin's "How the Book of Mormon Reads the Bible: A Theory of Types." Such essays show the merits of close reading through rhetorical, formalist, and narratological lenses. The *Journal of Book of Mormon Studies* is published by BYU's Neal A. Maxwell Institute (along with the University of Illinois Press) and so tends to feature authors from within the faith tradition. But the development of a strong literary angle on the Book of Mormon has been striking in Book of Mormon studies in part because it's drawn strong contributions from outside the Latter-day Saint faith and from outside the Latter-day Saint publishing world.

Particularly important in setting the tone for the larger 2010s literary conversation about the Book of Mormon were two essays published in 2013–14: Elizabeth Fenton's "Open Canons: Sacred History and Lay American History in *The Book of Mormon*" (published in *J19: The Journal*

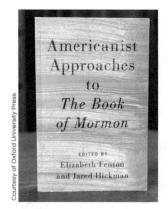

Americanist Approaches to "The Book of Mormon"

of Nineteenth-Century Americanists) and Jared Hickman's "*The Book of Mormon* as Amerindian Apocalypse" (published in *American Literature*). Dramatically more theoretical in nature than literary studies published in traditional Latter-day Saint outlets, Fenton's and Hickman's essays offered new readings of the text, but they also functioned as a call to theoretically and historically inclined Americanists to look seriously at the Book of Mormon. Hickman was soon directing a PhD dissertation at Johns Hopkins University with a serious treatment of the Book of Mormon, while Fenton was teaching a graduate seminar on the Book of Mormon at the University of Vermont. In 2018 the *Journal of Book of Mormon Studies* published an interview with Fenton about her seminar, along with a selection of papers produced by students in the seminar. Then, in 2019, Fenton and Hickman published an edited collection of essays of immense importance. Issued by Oxford University Press and entitled *Americanist Approaches to "The Book of Mormon,"* this volume marks a first culmination for literary criticism and the Book of Mormon. The book brings together seventeen essays analyzing the Book of Mormon from various literary and historical approaches, indicating the new acceptance of the Book of Mormon into the academy.

On its own turf, literary theory encompasses a number of complementary and competing theoretical methods: New Historicism, narratology, structuralism, poststructuralism, formalism, deconstruction, rhetorical criticism, feminist theory, postcolonialism, reader-response theory, and many more. Consequently, applications of literary theory to the Book of Mormon have only begun to appear. Since the 1980s, literary criticism's vast range of possibilities and diverse set of questions have reinvigorated biblical studies, and volumes like *Understanding the Book of Mormon* and especially *Americanist Approaches to "The Book of Mormon"* show that these possibilities and questions can and likely will do the same for Book of Mormon studies.

INTERTEXTUALITY

A fourth major area in Book of Mormon studies groups together several different kinds of study, all having to do with the study of the Book of Mormon's relationship to other sacred texts (especially the Bible). Although the word *intertextuality* has come into use in Book of Mormon studies only recently, it nicely covers these various dimensions of research, some of which have been going on for decades longer than others. *Intertextuality*, simply put, is a name for relationships between different texts, and intertextual study thus asks whether there are themes, characters, or ideas common to two distinct (sacred) texts. Commonality may imply deliberate dependence, but it doesn't have to imply any more than suggestive interaction in the mind of a reader. In biblical studies, naturally, intertextual research most commonly involves considering how New Testament authors use Old Testament texts in their writings—something that, unsurprisingly, has deepened understandings of the New Testament in remarkable ways. In Book of Mormon studies, intertextual research usually takes one of two forms. A first focuses on how the Book of Mormon adopts and adapts language, characteristics, and ideas from the Bible, whether the Old Testament or the New Testament. A second form, though, asks about how the Book of Mormon interacts (or at least might be compared) with major religious texts from faith traditions outside Christianity.

> **DEFINITION**
>
> *Intertextuality:*
> In the study of scripture, intertextuality refers to relationships of interaction between a volume of scripture and some other text. In Book of Mormon studies, this usually concerns the relationship between the Book of Mormon and the Bible. (The study of how one Book of Mormon author refers to the words of another is called "intratextuality.")

For a century, most of what was said about the Book of Mormon and the Bible was either that they confirmed and bolstered each other (the position of believers) or that the one shamelessly plagiarized the other (the position of unbelievers). Talk of either sort tended to focus on the evidence that the Book of Mormon is written in the same style and diction as the King James Bible and that it contains lengthy quotations from Isaiah, Malachi, and the Sermon on the Mount (all largely corresponding to the King James Version). These facts have played a role from the beginning in research on Book of Mormon translation, and they've also been important to literary study of the Book of Mormon. Further, though, they've called for attention in their own right as a focus of a kind of subdiscipline all their own.

Sidney Sperry laid important groundwork for a more sustained study of the Book of Mormon's relationship to the Bible—and to the King James Bible in particular. Sperry classified and then tackled head-on some of the more complex questions posed by the Book of Mormon's intertextual relationship with the Bible. He was the first to bring biblical scholarship to bear on the question of the Isaiah chapters in the Book of Mormon. Because many biblical scholars date parts of Isaiah (as well as its larger shape) to the sixth and fifth centuries before Christ, some have raised questions about whether these parts could have been included in brass plates taken from Jerusalem before the city's capture by Babylon around 586 BC. Sperry's approach to this issue, questioning the assumptions of some biblical scholars, proved deeply influential; it still appears in the writings of some scholars addressing the issue. Sperry also formed an influential answer to questions about the presence of New Testament language throughout the Book of Mormon. Sperry argued that New Testament and Book of Mormon authors had independent access to common sources that provided them with similar language. Hugh Nibley furthered and deepened Sperry's approach to this issue in his own work.

ISAIAH CHAPTERS AND THEIR EQUIVALENTS IN THE BOOK OF MORMON

Isaiah 2–14	=	2 Nephi 12–24
Isaiah 29	=	2 Nephi 26–27
Isaiah 48–49	=	1 Nephi 20–21
Isaiah 50–52	=	2 Nephi 7–8
Isaiah 53	=	Mosiah 15
Isaiah 54	=	3 Nephi 22

Less reactive and more provocative approaches to these issues came later, and they came from scholars outside the Latter-day Saint tradition. Philosopher Truman G. Madsen invited important biblical scholars to visit BYU in the 1970s, asking them to speak about the Book of Mormon in light of their own expertise. The resulting essays were published by BYU's own Religious Studies Center in 1978, and they remain refreshingly insightful almost half a century later. James H. Charlesworth's contribution focused on how the Book of Mormon's notion of the Messiah compares and contrasts with Jewish texts from the centuries just before Jesus Christ's birth. But especially important was Krister Stendahl's treatment of the Sermon on the Mount in the Book of Mormon. Stendahl pointed to subtle differences between the Book of Mormon and biblical versions of the sermon, noting how the differences bring the sermon from the Gospel of Matthew into conversation with the Gospel of John. Stendahl's approach thus largely set aside questions of what the connections with the Bible suggested about authorship or historicity and instead focused on how the intertextual connections, closely analyzed, revealed something about the text's meaning.

The potential fruits of this kind of approach unfortunately didn't really begin to appear until the twenty-first century. An important exception was Philip L. Barlow's *Mormons and the Bible*, published in 1991, which dedicated a chapter to assessing the uses of biblical language in the Book of Mormon. Barlow's book remains today the standard survey of the basic issues, with helpful data and a balanced discussion. The 1980s and 1990s were mostly given, though, to the debates between FARMS and Signature Books scholars that circled around whether Sperry's and Nibley's treatments of the Book of Mormon's relationship to the Bible were defensible. At times, as in the late 1990s FARMS volume *Isaiah in the Book of Mormon*, discussion of intertextual issues moved beyond debate to genuine clarification and interpretation of the meaning of the text. Generally, however, the conversation remained where it had already been before Stendahl or Barlow. Especially important, then, in shifting things definitively onto new terrain was Grant Hardy's *Understanding the Book of Mormon*. Hardy refused to offer simple solutions to the presence of New Testament language or potentially problematic Isaiah texts. He outlined ways believers might make sense of such intertextual relationships without compromising their faith, but he insisted that more would come from asking about what the Book of Mormon's interactions with the Bible do for the meaning of the text rather than for its relationship to history. Hardy's book, though, doesn't simply call for a new approach; it models it, and to remarkable effect. Showing that the Book of Mormon can be read as creatively adapting

> "The Book of Mormon narrative bulges with biblical expressions. More than fifty thousand phrases of three or more words, excluding definite and indefinite articles, are common to the Bible and the Book of Mormon."
>
> —Philip L. Barlow, *Mormons and the Bible: The Place of the Latter-day Saints in American Religion*

biblical language, he has pressed intertextual relationships into the service of something approaching theology.

In Hardy's wake, the twenty-first century's second decade has witnessed major developments in research on the Book of Mormon's interaction with biblical texts. Joseph M. Spencer's *The Vision of All* has undertaken a serious theological investigation of the uses of Isaiah in Nephi's record. Acknowledging the importance of historical questions about Isaiah but prioritizing textual meaning, he has shown how much has remained unasked during decades of wrangling over historical issues. Similar in spirit but focused on the presence of New Testament language in the Book of Mormon is Nicholas J. Frederick's work. In a major book-length study, *The Bible, Mormon Scripture, and the Rhetoric of Allusivity*, and several essays published in the *Journal of Book of Mormon Studies*, Frederick has examined the rhetorical functions played by New Testament language in the Book of Mormon. Further, though, he has revealed with particular force how inventively Book of Mormon texts interact with New Testament texts—breaking the dichotomy between supposedly slavish plagiarism of biblical sources and supposedly slavish dependence on ancient (but unknown) sources. Frederick's work thus, like Hardy's, pushes for recognizing deeper theological significance in how the Book of Mormon interacts with the Bible. Developments by Hardy, Spencer, and Frederick suggest that only the first stirring of serious intertextual work on the Bible and the Book of Mormon has yet occurred.

While most intertextual work has focused on the Bible and the Book of Mormon, several recent studies draw attention to what might be learned from setting the Book of Mormon alongside key religious texts from, for example, Islam or Hinduism. Such work is very new and thus largely untheorized. Part of the purpose in studying the Book of Mormon side by side with other scriptural texts is to reveal potentially similar teachings and clarify real differences. Particularly important in laying the foundation for future study is Grant Hardy's "The Book of Mormon as Post-Canonical Scripture." This essay compares the Book of Mormon with other (relatively) recently canonized works of world scripture and argues that the Book of Mormon, like them, advocates for a reopening of a closed canon. This is what the Adi Granth does for Islam's Qur'an and what the Book of Mormon does for the Bible. A more involved example of comparative scripture that involves the Book of Mormon can be found in the Maronite Catholic scholar Jad Hatem's book *Postponing Heaven: The Three Nephites, the Bodhisattva, and the Mahdi*, a study that veers strongly in the direction of theology or even philosophy of religion. The book compares the "human messianicity" (the religious disposition to save others) of the Book of Mormon's "Three Nephites" with the bodhisattvas of Mahayana Buddhism and the Mahdi figure in Twelver Shi'ite Islam. Hatem's work highlights how the story of the Three Nephites can be understood as presenting something more salvific and theologically approachable than has been suspected.

Two recent publications in the *Journal of Book of Mormon Studies* also deserve mention for helping pave the way for intertextual study of the Book of Mormon alongside world scripture. The first, Joseph Spencer's "Christ and Krishna: The Visions of Arjuna and the Brother of Jared," looks at the story of the brother of Jared side by side with that of Arjuna from the Hindu sacred text the Bhagavad Gita. Spencer argues that a comparison of the two allows for a better appreciation of the revolutionary nature of the brother of Jared's story. The second study, D. Morgan Davis's "Prophets and Prophecy in the Qur'an and the Book of Mormon," compares the prophetologies of the two texts. (A prophetology is a theory of what makes a prophet.) Davis's article also does important work in theorizing comparative scripture for Latter-day Saints. Articles like these, however, mostly demonstrate that scholars have only just begun to scratch the surface of comparative work on the Book of Mormon and other religious texts.

THEOLOGICAL INTERPRETATION

A fifth area of research in Book of Mormon studies has a more complex backstory than others. In certain ways, theology is the oldest lens through which the Book of Mormon has been viewed—already used by W. W. Phelps and Orson Pratt in the 1830s and 1840s. Lay and even semiprofessional theological reflection on the Book of Mormon prevailed through the nineteenth century into the twentieth. But with the intensification of historical interest in the Book of Mormon—in and after Fawn Brodie's biography—theological reflection on the Book of Mormon largely halted. It's ironic that the very same decades that saw the retreat of theology from Book of Mormon studies also saw the emergence of an intense program of "biblical theology" in biblical studies. Something of the same spirit that animated Christian biblical theology, however, arguably found its way into the Latter-day Saint context. This took place in what O. Kendall White Jr. has called the neo-orthodox moment in Latter-day Saint history. Growing out of Joseph Fielding Smith's writings but coming especially into focus in the books and sermons of Elder Bruce R. McConkie, this moment involved an intense interest in *doctrine*. Although without training in theology or philosophy (or the history of Christianity), doctrinal thinkers and scholars drew from commonsense readings of scripture and of the teachings of Latter-day Saint authorities to construct an overarching theological picture of the Restoration.

The doctrinal framework constructed in the mid-twentieth century soon became a lens for viewing scripture. Beginning with Elder McConkie's own three-volume *Doctrinal New Testament Commentary*, a style of interpretation developed that read texts largely to confirm the truth of the larger doctrinal schema of those texts. In the unstable 1980s—when literary readings of the Book of Mormon came under suspicion and reasoned defense of the Book of Mormon's antiquity became particularly intense—religious educators at BYU found stability by transferring Elder McConkie's program of interpretation from the New Testament to the Book of

DEFINITION

Theology:
In the broadest sense, theology is simply reasoned reflection on God or on revelation. Practically speaking, there are many different approaches to theological interpretation of scripture, including the Book of Mormon.

Mormon. In annual symposia (later published as collections of essays), BYU's Religious Studies Center gathered doctrinally minded scholars to read the Book of Mormon. Doctrinal scholarship in Elder McConkie's wake was uninterested in intellectual novelty or in simply adding to the encyclopedia of knowledge. It exhibited a spirit of loyalty rather than individuality as it wove deliberately devotional insights into doctrinal exposition. The approach was thus simultaneously learned and yet aimed at nonscholars in a particularly successful way.

The doctrinal program of interpreting the Book of Mormon came to a kind of first culmination with the four-volume *Doctrinal Commentary on the Book of Mormon*, primarily written by BYU religious educators Robert L. Millet and Joseph Fielding McConkie (the latter of whom was Elder McConkie's son). Other doctrinal studies of the Book of Mormon would follow, along with other doctrinal commentaries (such as Monte S. Nyman's six-volume *Book of Mormon Commentary* or D. Kelly Ogden and Andrew C. Skinner's two-volume *Verse by Verse: The Book of Mormon*). From its beginning to the end of the twentieth century, such doctrinal study of the Book of Mormon proceeded without its adherents seeking training in theology or philosophy. The first decades of the twenty-first century, however, saw a tightly knit group of theological interpreters emerge—with a particular focus on the Book of Mormon—united by their training in these and closely related fields (such as literary theory).

Gathered around James E. Faulconer, a BYU philosophy professor with deep interests in philosophy of religion and the theory of interpretation, several of these young philosophers and theologians launched the Mormon Theology Seminar in 2008 (later renamed the Latter-day Saint Theology Seminar) and then Salt Press in 2011 (later absorbed into the Neal A. Maxwell Institute). The first volume published by the Seminar, focused on readings of Alma 32, opens with a manifesto of sorts that distinguishes theological interpretation from both historical research and doctrinal study. Especially important to this interpretive

DEFINITION

Neo-orthodoxy:
A movement in early twentieth-century Christianity that resisted strongly optimistic visions of human capabilities and emphasized the role of grace in salvation. It has been argued that the Latter-day Saint tradition had its own neo-orthodox moment.

project is a distinction between theology and doctrine. Doctrine, editor Adam S. Miller explains, is authoritative, decided and announced by leaders of the Church. By contrast, theology is deliberately academic and speculative, addressing questions of interest to the life of faith but of little or no institutional importance. Gathering at Seminar symposia—as well as at conferences organized by the Society for Mormon Philosophy and Theology, the Association of Mormon Scholars in the Humanities, and eventually the Book of Mormon Studies Association—Latter-day Saint scriptural theologians began in the early 2010s to lay the foundations for a recognizable subdiscipline.

The first single-authored book in the strictly theological vein was Joseph Spencer's *An Other Testament: On Typology*, a study that explicitly distances itself from Nibley's historical program and Hardy's literary program. Informed by both of these other disciplines but asking a different set of questions, Spencer's work brings the Book of Mormon into conversation with major philosophical and theological questions (in particular, the question "What does it mean to read a text spiritually?"). Spencer's book, moreover, opened a book series published by BYU's Maxwell Institute starting in 2016, to which were soon added Jad Hatem's comparative study of the Book of Mormon alongside Buddhism and Islam (*Postponing Heaven*) and David Charles Gore's rhetorical-theological study of political discourse in the Book of Mormon (*The Voice of the People*). And similar developments were occurring elsewhere. About the same time that Spencer's book appeared in the Maxwell Institute series, John Christopher Thomas's *A Pentecostal Reads the Book of Mormon: A Literary and Theological Introduction* appeared, showing the interest that theological readings of the text can have for those outside the faith.

By the end of the 2010s, theological studies had begun appearing in journals both inside and outside the Latter-day Saint publishing context. Notable examples are Kimberly Matheson Berkey's "Temporality and Fulfillment in 3 Nephi 1" and Rosalynde Frandsen Welch's "Lehi's Brass Ball: Astonishment and Inscription," both published in the *Journal of Book of Mormon Studies*, and Nicholas J. Frederick and Joseph M. Spencer's "John 11 in the Book of Mormon," published in the *Journal of the Bible and Its Reception*. Another important publishing endeavor for theological reading of the Book of Mormon has been the output of the already-mentioned Latter-day Saint Theology Seminar. To date, volumes have appeared on Alma 32; 2 Nephi 26–27; 1 Nephi 1; Jacob 7; and Alma 12–13, with volumes forthcoming on Mosiah 15 and Mosiah 4. Perhaps most important, however, is the 2020 publication of a twelve-volume series of theological studies by the Maxwell Institute, marking a first culmination for theological research on the Book of Mormon. *The Book of Mormon: Brief Theological Introductions* features twelve different authors, each assigned a part of the Book of Mormon to address in a deliberately theological way. Featuring thinkers trained in philosophy, early Christian history, literature, and theology proper (ranging from Terryl Givens to David F. Holland and from Deidre Nicole Green to Rosalynde Frandsen Welch), the series clearly shows that theology has become an important contributor to Book of Mormon studies.

RECEPTION HISTORY

A sixth area of active research in Book of Mormon studies has a less complicated prehistory and represents an angle on the text as new as the theological. This is the work of studying reception history. The field of reception history—of tracing the ways people have received, appropriated, and used scriptural texts throughout history—is relatively new even in biblical scholarship, but its arrival in Book of Mormon scholarship can be said to have only a few traces before the twenty-first century. There have been reviews of the literature from the beginning of Book of Mormon studies, but reception history is a different beast. Reception historians analyze how scripture has functioned in scholarship but also in authoritative religious sermons and teaching curricula, art and literature, advertising and merchandizing, politics and scientific discourse, historiography and everything else. Aiming to understand how changing interpretations of the Book of Mormon reveal its significance, the reception historian locates these in specific cultural and historical frameworks. Since the possibilities for studying the reception history of scriptures are ever increasing, scholars have to decide with care whose responses are important for study, how to justify their choice of materials, and what methods to employ in analysis.

Early studies of the reception of the Book of Mormon focused on institutional concerns—for example, on how Church leaders have used the Book of Mormon in their writing and preaching. Seminal essays on this topic were Grant Underwood's "Book of Mormon Usage in Early LDS Theology" and Noel B. Reynolds's "The Coming Forth of the Book of Mormon in the Twentieth Century." Analyzing all major Church periodicals published before 1846, as well as numerous tracts, pamphlets, and journals, Underwood found that the Saints' earliest uses of the Book of Mormon were primarily eschatological (focused on end times) and fit a nineteenth-century millenarian worldview. His most cited finding is that early Saints quoted the Bible twenty times more frequently than the Book of Mormon. This data point was instrumental in establishing the now-common understanding that the Book of Mormon has functioned for the Saints from the beginning largely as a sign of Joseph Smith's prophetic status. In his study, Reynolds sifted institutional records—especially those connected to BYU—to show that the Book of Mormon only slowly came to cultural prominence over the course of the twentieth century. Other important early studies of reception history, most published in the *Journal of Book of Mormon Studies*, concerned the history of the English Book of Mormon's translation into a variety of languages for use by missionaries.

Terryl L. Givens's 2002 *By the Hand of Mormon* proved to be a flash point for reception history. Givens took Underwood's and Reynolds's arguments for granted and built on them a large-scale history of the intellectual reception of the Book of Mormon. Givens traced the history of attacks on, as well as defenses of, the Book of Mormon's historicity. That a major academic press published *By the Hand of Mormon* immediately drew serious attention to Givens's argument, deepening the impression made by earlier research on the basic contours of the Book of Mormon's reception history. Part of the impact of Givens's study, however, lay in generating closer scrutiny of just how representative early Church periodicals were of the Book of Mormon's

> **DEFINITION**
>
> *Eschatology:*
> Reflection on the end of history, which in Christian contexts includes themes like the Second Coming of Jesus Christ, the dawn of a millennium of peace, the gathering of scattered Israel, and so on.

role in the early Saints' lives. Several scholars have accordingly pushed back against Givens, noting how the Book of Mormon influenced early efforts at Church organization and theology and Joseph Smith's early social and political thought.

Leading the way in nuancing the early history of the reception of the Book of Mormon has been Janiece Johnson's work, beginning with "Becoming a People of the Books: Toward an Understanding of Early Mormon Converts and the New Word of the Lord." Published in the *Journal of Book of Mormon Studies* in 2018, this essay focuses on the private writings of early converts and shows that early Church members used the Book of Mormon much as they did the Bible. They turned to it less often than the Bible, but it was a regular part of devotional practice and a ready resource for self-understanding. Amy Easton-Flake's work is also important in this regard. Easton-Flake has looked carefully at how members of the Church used scripture at the end of the nineteenth century in both personal and public writings. Together, Johnson's and Easton-Flake's work has begun to alter a long-received picture. It has also disclosed substantial differences between how women and men have employed the Book of Mormon in the Church's history.

The fact that Givens used reception history to approach the Book of Mormon certainly played a role in making his study of interest to Oxford University Press. At any rate, the possibilities for bridging the distance between those inside and outside the faith tradition through reception history became suddenly clear with Givens's successful study. Paul C. Gutjahr's *The Book of Mormon: A Biography* accordingly soon followed, another broad reception history of the Book of Mormon but one written by a non–Latter-day Saint. Gutjahr's book demonstrates in a way that Givens's doesn't the range that reception studies can have. It includes chapters on missionary work, scholarship, art and illustration, film and theater, and the translation of the text into non-English languages. Indebted to Givens and Gutjahr alike, reception history work in the 2010s quickly proliferated. Representative articles appeared in the *Journal of Book of Mormon Studies*, including J. David Pulsipher's "Buried Swords: The Shifting Interpretive Ground of a Beloved Book of Mormon Narrative"; Christopher James Blythe's "'A Very Fine Azteck Manuscript': Latter-day Saint Readings of Codex Boturini"; and

Rebekah Westrup's "Imaginings of the Book of Mormon: A Comparison of Arnold Friberg's and Minerva Teichert's Book of Mormon Paintings." The 2021 issue of the *Journal of Book of Mormon Studies*, moreover, has been dedicated to sustained reflections on major aspects of the history of Book of Mormon studies as a field.

Book of Mormon reception history is of course still in its infancy. The larger contours of the Book of Mormon's history of interpretation have been traced only in rough outline, providing only a first approximation. And detailed studies of aspects of the Book of Mormon's reception have appeared for only a few contexts. But because reception history —like literary study and to some extent theology—is removed from debates over historicity, it has particular promise for appealing to an audience of outsiders as much as to an audience of insiders. What's clearest, though, is that the vast majority of reception history work remains undone. Potential studies in this vein of scholarship are limitless, and they're crying for attention. Students of the subject may choose to consider how the Book of Mormon functions in contexts ranging from the tracts of nineteenth-century apocalyptic religious factions to the twenty-first-century production of action figures, from long-forgotten curriculum materials early in the twentieth century to personal devotional practices among working mothers in the international Church at the end of the twentieth century. Further, reception history points the way toward a field of Book of Mormon scholarship more invested in and aware of a wide range of readers, studying a book that sits in the hands of an increasingly diverse readership.

IDEOLOGY CRITIQUE

A final area of research in Book of Mormon studies concerns questions of diversity. Book of Mormon scholarship has followed a historical trajectory that's similar to that of other disciplines in at least one crucial way. As the number of scholars from traditionally underrepresented demographics and diverse disciplinary backgrounds has increased, the contours of the field have changed in important ways. Thus, the last couple of decades have witnessed, alongside other developments, increasing interest in topics like disability, gender, race, postcolonialism, social justice, and the Book of Mormon's relation to other religious texts. There has also been an increase in what scholars call "ideological" approaches to studying the Book of Mormon—that is, research that deliberately examines the text from the perspective of a particular social group, intentionally attentive to that group's concerns and commitments. These methods of interpretation take seriously the notion that scripture is a living text, a text to be likened to the individual circumstances and the concerns of all its readers, wherever and whenever they live.

First stirrings of readings along these lines can be traced once more to Hugh Nibley, whose speeches and writings on the Book of Mormon from the late 1960s onward (and especially during the 1980s) largely left off addressing historical issues in order to ask about the political and economic relevance of the Book of Mormon. Other readers followed suit in the wake of the social upheavals of the 1960s—among them John Sorenson (on racial matters) and Eugene England (on racial matters and also on questions of violence). A particularly important example of such readings somewhat later in the twentieth century is the handful of feminist interpreters who began writing about women in the Book of Mormon. Some of these hoped to defend the book against charges of misogyny (such as Jerrie W. Hurd, Francine R. Bennion, and Camille S. Williams), while others concluded that the book is ultimately patriarchal (such as Carol Lynn Pearson and Lynn Matthews Anderson). All, however, contributed in crucial ways to questions that have become only more prominent in the twenty-first century. Racial issues were less consistent than gender issues in drawing attention among Book of Mormon scholars during the last decades of the twentieth century, despite certain important contributions. This seems to be because other parts of Latter-day Saint scripture (especially the Book of Abraham) and history drew the bulk of attention concerning race.

Really, though, the broadening of these important concerns into a wider range of ethical motivations for interpreting the Book of Mormon had to wait for the twenty-first century. Recently, interest in these and many related issues has expanded dramatically. Blair Dee Hodges's "A Disability Studies Reading of Moroni Chapter 8" is, for example, the very first study of its kind. Hodges examines the Book of Mormon's treatment of infant baptism in light of concerns regarding baptizing individuals with intellectual or developmental disabilities. His essay argues that

> "The strength and beauty of a holy text is that it can be read again and again, with different and new understandings and insights revealed every time. A holy text is not exhausted by a single interpretation; it compels readers to return and review, reexamine, and reinterpret."
>
> —Fatimah Salleh and Margaret Olsen Hemming, *The Book of Mormon for the Least of These*, vol. 1, 1 Nephi–Words of Mormon

because baptism serves more functions in the Book of Mormon than representing or activating a remission of sins, people with disabilities might more often be included rather than prohibited from participating in the practice. For such individuals, baptism might function primarily as an adoptive ordinance, which would symbolically welcome them into the family of Saints. Hodges has opened the door for the possibility of disability research in the Book of Mormon, but that door has been open for such a short time so far that it remains unclear how soon other scholars will walk through.

Much more work has appeared in recent years about race and gender in the Book of Mormon. A particularly forceful and novel approach to questions of race in the book appeared in Jared Hickman's 2014 "*The Book of Mormon* as Amerindian Apocalypse," an important literary contribution as well as a reflection on race in the book. Hickman argues that the Book of Mormon indeed contains a problematic and worrisome portrayal of race but also that it contains a deliberate critique of that same portrayal of race. The book thus, in Hickman's terms, undertakes a "metacritique" of racism and racialism that's of interest far beyond simplistic yes-or-no questions about whether the Book of Mormon is racist. Hickman's approach has rapidly become generative, shaping much that's been published in the past decade—for example, Peter Coviello's treatment of race and the secular in *Make Yourselves Gods: Mormons and the Unfinished Business of American Secularism*.

A similar argument about the Book of Mormon, but one that's focused more on gender than on race, has appeared in Kimberly

Minerva Teichert (1888–1976), *Love Story*, 1949–1951, oil on masonite, 36 x 48 inches. Brigham Young University Museum of Art, 1969.

Matheson Berkey and Joseph M. Spencer's 2019 essay "'Great Cause to Mourn': The Complexity of *The Book of Mormon*'s Presentation of Gender and Race." Berkey and Spencer argue that the Book of Mormon resists misogyny in something like the way it problematizes race: by portraying a devastating history of violence toward women but then including important prophetic critiques of that history. In her contribution to the 2020 *The Book of Mormon: Brief Theological Introductions* series, Deidre Green made a similar argument at greater length and with further nuance. Arguing that the Book of Mormon might be an asset rather than a liability when it comes to pushing for real equality between the sexes, Green portrays a book of scripture that's of deep relevance in the twenty-first century. These contributions are, though, just a sampling of what's happened in recent years. Recognizing the need for more visibility of good work on these topics, the editors of the *Journal of Book of Mormon Studies* have helpfully published detailed reviews of the literature on the Book of Mormon and race (in the 2018 issue) and on the Book of Mormon and gender (in the 2020 issue).

The past two decades have also played host to a fusion of reception studies with interest in politically complex issues. A good example is Stanley J. Thayne's essay "'We're Going to Take Our Land Back Over': Indigenous Positionality, the Ethnography of Reading, and *The Book of Mormon*." Thayne's essay draws attention to the ways that a citizen of the Catawba Indian Nation reads and understands the Book of Mormon. It thus provides an interpretation of the text that scholars easily miss because of their social locations and ideological perspectives. Similar work has appeared from Elise Boxer ("The Book of Mormon as Mormon Settler Colonialism"), Farina King ("Indigenizing Mormonisms"), Thomas W. Murphy ("Other Scriptures: Restoring Voices of Gantowisas to an Open Canon"), and Hayes Peter Mauro (*Messianic Fulfillments: Staging Indigenous Salvation in America*). Yet another question in which reception studies has productively fused with moral and political concerns is violence. Recent work, especially work by J. David Pulsipher and Patrick Q. Mason, considers the history of how Latter-day Saints have read the Book of Mormon's more violent episodes—such as Nephi's killing of Laban and Captain Moroni's management of long wars—and asks how changing interpretations might assist in promoting a nonviolent reading of the Book of Mormon.

Review of Books on the Book of Mormon and *Journal of Book of Mormon Studies*

Still other works attend to issues of social justice more broadly, such as Todd M. Compton's essay "The Spirituality of the Outcast in the Book of Mormon." A particularly noteworthy recent publication of this sort is Fatima Salleh and Margaret Olsen Hemming's *The Book of Mormon for the Least of These*, a commentary in several volumes (although only the first volume has as yet appeared). Authored by trained scholars but written to reach nonspecialist audiences, the book explores the first seven books of the Book of Mormon for messages about inequality, oppression, anti-racism, nonviolence, and other issues relating to social justice. The volume differs significantly from previous Book of Mormon commentaries in that its primary interests aren't doctrinal, historical, or literary aspects of the text. Rather, Salleh and Hemming's goal has been to help readers work against oppression and see the world through the lens of a gospel in which the first will be last and the last first. The commentary brings into focus and provides a center of gravity for decades of scattered reflections on what it means to read the Book of Mormon with an eye to social justice, ensuring that the text can be scripture for all readers. It turns the interpretive kaleidoscope, allowing readers to view the text from different angles and perspectives. Indeed, all the work gathered under this final category of Book of Mormon research evaluates and critiques often unacknowledged assumptions of both scriptural authors and traditional interpreters of their writings.

* * *

For each of the subdisciplines that make up the field of Book of Mormon studies, there is an interesting and informative prehistory behind the current conversation. Also, though, over the past two decades, the field has matured and developed in significant ways in all its subdisciplines. There is every reason for scholars to press forward in each of these different areas of principal interest. There is especially good reason for them to do so while being deeply informed about the good work that has been done and thoroughly aware of the most recent developments in the field. Too often a lack of awareness of others' work has marred otherwise productive research by people working in Book of Mormon studies. This can be easily improved with conscious effort and greater access to past research. It is, however, only one of many obstacles facing the discipline.

| CHAPTER 3 |

Overcoming Obstacles

From all we've said so far, it should be apparent that the field of Book of Mormon studies not only has a fascinating and sometimes fraught past but also has a good many promising prospects as it looks to the future. The survey in the last chapter points to the fact that there are genuinely new things stirring today. The twentieth century's consistently dominant emphasis on historical research—whether critical toward or defensive of the Book of Mormon's antiquity—has become only a part, and really a relatively small part, of the field in the twenty-first century. Literary and theological approaches have freed themselves from former constraints and become major contributors. Reception history and intertextuality, almost without precedent, have arisen to become particularly important parts of the growing field. Political, ethical, and ideological questions have broadened dramatically, with unanticipated answers to old questions appearing. Even the story of the coming forth of the Book of Mormon has been set on wholly new footing in the last decade or two. It seems safe to say that the field of Book of Mormon studies today would be largely unrecognizable to someone visiting from the 1950s using a time machine. It would even be largely unrecognizable to someone visiting from the 1980s or 1990s.

Change is never easy, however, and massive, rapid change is especially hard. And as we overviewed in the last chapter, the changes that have taken place in Book of Mormon studies are as massive as they've been quick. We don't need to imagine time machines to think about how today's field would look to someone shaped by the late twentieth century's version of Book of Mormon studies. Many people right now who were shaped by this version express surprise at what has happened and what's happening now. For some, the changes are welcome and exhilarating. For others, they're confusing but interesting. For others still, they're downright alarming. All these reactions are understandable. *They're also all important.* Younger scholars in Book of Mormon studies must learn as much from the older generation's expressions of concern as from its words of encouragement. This is partly because change isn't hard just for more seasoned individuals who see familiar forms of things pass away. Change is also hard in its own way for those who are born into or shaped by the new. One unfortunate limitation for those not influenced by the old is the potential to be blind to real dangers that lurk in the new. This blinding can lead them to ignore the sage advice of those who have seen the old and the new.

We'll dwell on all that more in a moment as we examine closely what obstacles Book of Mormon studies faces. First, though, it's worth addressing one particularly important and instructive indication that something fundamentally new is happening in Book of Mormon studies. It's insufficient just to point out that the interests and approaches garnering the most attention in the field find little or only scattered precedent in previous decades. It isn't terribly surprising that what shaped the 2000s and 2010s isn't the same as what influenced the 1980s or the 1990s (let alone the 1950s and 1960s). What *is* surprising—and especially telling—is that the first decades of the twenty-first century have seen a return to the methods of the decades that *preceded* the 1950s. In crucial ways, we've returned to the formative period of Book of Mormon studies—but with professional and genuinely academic tools.

In previous chapters, we talked about Book of Mormon studies as having really begun with the emergence of academically trained scholars

Overcoming Obstacles

in the 1940s. The field began to take shape as a recognizable discipline only with the seminal work of Sidney B. Sperry, M. Wells Jakeman, and especially Hugh W. Nibley. It was on these three scholars' shoulders that later twentieth-century Book of Mormon scholars stood when they watched over the growth and development of the field. But Sperry, Jakeman, and Nibley didn't work in an intellectual vacuum. As we mentioned in chapter 1, serious and productive readers and interpreters of the Book of Mormon worked influentially from the late 1870s into the 1940s. They were, strictly speaking, amateurs, but one should highlight the etymological meaning of "amateur": *lover*. They were lovers of the Book of Mormon, and they lovingly plowed the field in which Sperry, Jakeman, and Nibley planted the seeds of the discipline. And today's Book of Mormon scholars —apart from the question of professional training—have more in common with those amateur students of the book than they do with the scholars that followed.

> **DEFINITION**
>
> Amateur:
> Literally, a lover of something, used to suggest someone who works for something out of love rather than out of professional obligation or with the aid of professional training.

Most important in this regard are figures like Orson Pratt, George Reynolds, Janne M. Sjödahl, and B. H. Roberts—figures we've already mentioned in previous chapters. What united these early students of the Book of Mormon was their focus on preliminary, ground-laying work. They didn't shy away from the thankless labor that *someone* had to do to make serious study of the Book of Mormon possible in the first place. Orson Pratt devoted untold hours to creating the first edition of the book that was geared specifically for study. George Reynolds produced the first well-received reference materials for Book of Mormon study. Janne Sjödahl's interpretive labors inspired his son-in-law to gather Sjödahl's writings into the first substantial commentary on the Book of Mormon. And B. H. Roberts undertook the first speculative interpretation of the entire book's meaning, which was audacious and in conversation with the science and theology of his day. Editions organized for careful study, substantial reference materials with reliable information, verse-by-verse commentaries to guide readers, and large-scale interpretations meant to generate real conversation—these are exactly the kinds of things required for a field of productive scriptural scholarship to thrive. They're also exactly the kinds of things scholars at the end of the twentieth century—and now in the first decades of the twenty-first century—have been attending to.

Orson Pratt's work on the 1879 edition of the Book of Mormon, discussed briefly in chapter 1, was the first of its kind. Elder Pratt received the assignment earlier that year to produce a new edition that devoted closer attention to the needs of readers. Accordingly, he divided the text into shorter chapter divisions, introduced versification into the text for the first time, and supplied the volume with its first cross-referential and even interpretive footnotes. Readers of the edition publicly celebrated its merits, commenting on the way its system of citation made study of the text more possible than before. Explanatory footnotes, along with footnotes containing inter- and intratextual references, gave readers a more intellectually engaged experience with the Book of Mormon. Elder Pratt felt the Saints' need for an edition of the Book of Mormon they could study—something that required a great expenditure of effort on his part, and he faithfully delivered it. The same need has apparently been felt—by a surprising number of people—late in the twentieth and early in the twenty-first century.

A page from the book of Omni in Orson Pratt's 1879 edition of the Book of Mormon.

Work that culminated in the most important twenty-first-century editions of the Book of Mormon began in the early 1980s with critical analysis of the book's print history. First headed up by Robert Smith, whose critical text appeared in the mid-1980s, the project eventually became the life's work of Royal Skousen. Skousen has carefully examined and reexamined the manuscripts (the original manuscript and a manu-

Study-focused editions of the Book of Mormon. Courtesy of Yale University Press, the University of Illinois Press, and the Neal A. Maxwell Institute for Religious Scholarship.

script copy used in printing, appropriately called the printer's manuscript), as well as every major print edition of the Book of Mormon. He's tracked all variants among these many versions of the text, analyzed them carefully, worked to place them in a larger linguistic framework, and published his detailed notes for all the world. The year 2009 saw the first major culmination of Skousen's monumental work: *The Book of Mormon: The Earliest Text* (ideally read alongside the six-volume *Analysis of Textual Variants of the Book of Mormon* that explains how every decision about *The Earliest Text* was made). Smith and Skousen were thus the first to seriously embrace the idea that progress in Book of Mormon studies depends on a textually reliable edition. The service they've provided deserves the gratitude of all Book of Mormon scholars.

As Skousen labored away on his project, other scholars began to express similar concerns about the readability of the Book of Mormon. Starting with Grant Hardy's *The Book of Mormon: A Reader's Edition*, various new editions of the Book of Mormon in the 2000s and 2010s have tried to make its shape and flow clearer for readers. To date, the most important of these is Hardy's 2018 *Maxwell Institute Study Edition*, which combines the best of Hardy's literary insights with the most important of Smith's and Skousen's discoveries. In all this work, Orson Pratt's spirit seems to hover nearby, always pressing for a more readable text. These developments mark an important return to the very beginnings of Book of Mormon research—a recognition that progress won't be made until the book's shape and flow are apparent and its meaning accessible.

Elder Pratt's 1879 edition made George Reynolds's labors to create Book of Mormon reference material possible (something Reynolds himself pointed out). Elder Pratt's citation systems (chapters and verses)

> "It is wonderful to me how much more interesting the study of the Book of Mormon has become since it has been divided into chapters and verses. I seem to get hold of the sense so much better than when it was in such long paragraphs."
>
> —George Reynolds, "Correspondence," *Millennial Star*, October 1879, 669

were certainly necessary before a concordance was possible. As Reynolds read the Orson Pratt edition, his study led him to produce *A Dictionary of the Book of Mormon*, a major systematization of Book of Mormon characters, places, and events. Going further, he then published *A Complete Concordance to the Book of Mormon*, a massive work that tabulated every word used in the Book of Mormon and took twenty-one years to complete. Reynolds essentially created these resources from scratch, with little by way of even amateur scholarship available to him. He nonetheless rightly saw that serious study of the Book of Mormon couldn't move forward without good and reliable reference materials. Scholars like Sperry, Jakeman, and Nibley couldn't have done their work without Reynolds's tools ready at hand.

Here again, twenty-first-century scholars are returning to the insights of the Book of Mormon's earliest students. Already in the late 1990s, the Foundation for Ancient Research and Mormon Studies (FARMS) published *A Comprehensive Annotated Book of Mormon Bibliography* (overseen by Donald W. Parry), *Charting the Book of Mormon* (principally the work of John W. Welch), and *The Geography of Book of Mormon Events* (the tireless effort of John L. Sorenson). To these important and preliminary reference works are joined many more resources created in the twenty-first century. Skousen's work on the critical text project has yielded some of the most important of these: his six-volume *Analysis of Textual Variants of the Book of Mormon* and seven-volume *History of the Text of the Book of Mormon*. Also important are the Joseph Smith Papers publications of the manuscript sources for the Book of Mormon, alongside web-based access to these manuscripts and other historically important editions of the book. Other twenty-first-century resources have focused on gathering and synthesizing past work. In 2003, for instance, Deseret Book published the *Book of Mormon Reference Companion*, edited by Dennis L. Largey, which surveys and summarizes Book of Mormon scholarship from the twentieth century. The online archive of Book of Mormon Central gathers much of this same scholarship in full (rather than in summary). More recently, Oxford University Press has published Larry E. Morris's *Documentary History of the Book of Mormon*, gathering into one place historical sources about the process of translating, publishing, and printing the Book of Mormon.

These new reference materials are indispensable, but it's worth pausing for a moment to state that they're only a start. Twentieth-century scholarship, as well as more recent scholarship, needs sifting to decide on its most lasting insights. Updates to the 1996 *Comprehensive Annotated Book of Mormon Bibliography* need to be made, and specialized literature reviews need to be written (some have in fact begun to appear in the *Journal of Book of Mormon Studies*). A full critical text of the Book of Mormon needs to appear, along with searchable versions of various historically important editions of the Book of Mormon. Dictionaries of word usage in the Book of Mormon would be of great value, ideally with entries that detail various possible meanings drawn from historical English and American usage. Systematic lists and preliminary analyses of intertextual connections between the Book of Mormon and the Bible, as well as between the Book of Mormon and other key Restoration texts, would help guide further work on the text. In short, the return of Reynolds's interest in producing reference material is more than welcome.

Often associated with George Reynolds is Janne Sjödahl, since their names appear together on the cover of the first multivolume commentary on the Book of Mormon ever published. But neither Reynolds nor Sjödahl set out to produce that commentary during their lifetimes, so it appeared only after their deaths. Sjödahl was a trained minister who joined The Church of Jesus Christ of Latter-day Saints and soon brought his theological learning to the task of reading the Book of Mormon. An indefatigable reader of the book, he piled up mounds of unpublished

> "Other than Joseph Smith and Oliver Cowdery, who are in a class unto themselves, Royal Skousen has done more to establish, correct, and elucidate the text of the Book of Mormon than anyone else in the history of the Church, including the first typesetter, John Gilbert; later editors such as Orson Pratt or James E. Talmage; and any number of commentators."
>
> —Grant Hardy, "Approaching Completion: The Book of Mormon Critical Text Project," *BYU Studies Quarterly* 57, no. 1 (2018): 179

reflections in addition to published articles and books over decades. After his death, his son-in-law Philip C. Reynolds—who also happened to be the son of George Reynolds—created from the two men's writings the first substantial verse-by-verse commentary on the Book of Mormon. The format of the commentary would prove deeply influential, shaping more or less all commentaries on the Book of Mormon published since.

Commentary on the Book of Mormon

The commentary that appeared under Sjödahl's and Reynolds's names was multifaceted, eschewing a single approach to the text. The era begun by Sperry, Jakeman, and Nibley that would center on the historicity of the Book of Mormon hadn't arrived yet. Further, the commentary appeared long before now-familiar interpretations of Book of Mormon passages settled. Even in the twenty-first century, then, the commentary often presents readers with novel and interesting approaches to the text, which speak to today's expanding field. In all these ways, the commentary is surprisingly akin to Brant A. Gardner's six-volume commentary on the Book of Mormon, *Second Witness*, published in 2007. And although Gardner's commentary privileges historical and archaeological approaches to the text (as Reynolds and Sjödahl's commentary did often enough), his commentary is as disciplinarily diverse as that of his earliest commentator forebears. Here as elsewhere, there's been a crucial return to the very beginnings of Book of Mormon scholarship, however amateur those beginnings were.

Second Witness

It's worth pausing briefly to say that Gardner's commentary should be just the beginning of a revitalized commentary tradition. Serious and substantial commentaries are a good place for sifting previous work. They're also good venues for novel approaches and systematic readings to appear. Ideally, however, commentaries on the Book of Mormon in the future will no longer represent the work of just one or two individuals. In biblical studies, few commentary series are sole authored. Rather, different scholars write on different biblical books—and often on just parts of different biblical books. Ideally, then, we'll soon see great commentaries on the Book of Mormon written by a dozen or more scholars, with one contributor writing a long and detailed study of 1 Nephi and another writing a long and detailed study of Helaman. (Something like this has already begun to appear with the Maxwell Institute's *The Book of Mormon: Brief Theological Introductions* series.)

What, finally, of B. H. Roberts? Roberts was a particularly important intellectual force in the early twentieth century, and he commanded reflection on the Book of Mormon for decades. What may have been most important about Roberts's approach to the book, though, was his attempt to provide the book with a total reading. In other words, Roberts constructed a framework for making sense of the whole Book of Mormon rather than simply of this or that passage. He put this larger framework in conversation, moreover, with the best theological and scientific research of his day. It's important to note at the same time, though, that the result of Roberts's particular research was actually a dead end. Too attached to his model, he didn't know how to deal with new data, and this actually threatened his long-standing faith in the Book of Mormon for a time. His work was nonetheless crucial and carried serious momentum in its time. With a more self-critical regard—or at least some conversation partners—he might have in fact represented an ideal interpreter of the Book of Mormon.[1]

Generally more cautious than Roberts was, recent interpreters of the Book of Mormon have also begun asking about the bearing of the whole book. Grant Hardy's *Understanding the Book of Mormon: A Reader's Guide*, Joseph Spencer's *An Other Testament: On Typology*, Brant Gardner's *Traditions of the Fathers: The Book of Mormon as History*, and Don Bradley's *The Lost 116 Pages: Reconstructing the Book of Mormon's Missing Stories*, among others, have attempted whole-book interpretations in just the past decade. Further, much recent literary and theological work on the Book of Mormon—even when it limits its insights to specific parts of the Book of Mormon—promises to contribute to proposals about the book's total meaning. Here again is something of a return to the beginnings of Book of Mormon studies, an attempt to recapture something perhaps lost during the later twentieth century. Such Roberts-like work is certainly in its infancy. What exists today is a loose collection of proposals, some more and some less worked out. The scholars setting forth these proposals need to encounter each other to provoke a sustained conversation, avoiding the temptation to write in so many individual echo chambers. Mirroring Roberts but also learning from his mistakes, work of this sort, which has only just begun, might well prove to be definitive for the twenty-first century.

Today's Book of Mormon scholars thus bring together the groundlaying intentions of early amateur Book of Mormon scholars and the professionalism of later trained Book of Mormon scholars. Conscious of how much preliminary work remains undone, current Book of Mormon scholars are building something with hope that it will last. Whether the result will be able to stand the test of time will be decided by the care with which this transitional and preliminary work is undertaken.

The watchword for the next several decades of Book of Mormon scholarship should therefore be *caution*. This, though, is a word too easily misunderstood—too easily taken to call for timidity or hesitance. The point isn't to warn that every step must be taken fearfully and flinchingly. It's rather to point out that success in this endeavor will be determined wholly by how thoroughly and undogmatically Book of Mormon scholars do their work. If dangers lurk in all directions, they're the dangers of laziness and dishonesty. Earlier scholarship can't be read from a position of ironic distance with a smirk about how naive earlier interpreters must have been. The textual data of the Book of Mormon has to be gathered and sorted and presented in solid reference works, which can't be done in a slipshod fashion or with any agendas about what the data will look like. Big-picture theories about how to understand the Book of Mormon as a whole can't be presented as if they are certain or decisive. It's in these kinds of ways that the cardinal virtue of Book of Mormon scholarship for the near future has to be caution. What's needed is unswerving commitment to intellectual humility and to real honesty, combined with the kind of patience and stamina necessary for doing preliminary (as well as not-so-preliminary) work well.

DEFINITION

Undogmatic:
Being unwilling to decide in advance what the evidence will prove; remaining honest and open in the task of investigation.

Caution will be as important for more traditional interpreters of the Book of Mormon as for those embracing newer methods or asking newer questions. Naturally, there are temptations in pursuing theological or literary work to push the text further in some interpretive direction than it can go—to uncritically adopt a sophisticated or fashionable theoretical lens even when it's a barrier to reading the text well. Similar temptations attend reception history and ideology critique. In asking questions about gender, race, and class or about violence, disability, and politics, it's easy to become tendentious. And so young scholars working in emerging subdisciplines in Book of Mormon studies need to exercise caution in pursuing their work.

But this doesn't mean that more traditional interpreters—shaped in the molds cast by twentieth-century Book of Mormon scholars—don't have as much need to exercise caution. Traditional defenses of the Book of Mormon have their own (and often unstated) theological, literary, and ideological commitments. Such work also faces the temptation to rigidly insist on its own theoretical frameworks, which are just as liable to obscure the text when they aren't the right tool for the interpretive job. And unfortunately, the pits traditional interpreters are most likely to fall into can be more difficult to see, if only because their methods are familiar and accepted. The result is that scholars embracing newer methods tend to see where traditional work makes unquestioned assumptions, just as scholars who productively persist in traditional methods tend to see where younger scholars let newfangled theories get the better of them. And so, to whatever extent Book of Mormon studies can become a place for generous conversation—a place for mutual assistance in avoiding blind spots rather than for rancorous accusations—its future looks wonderfully bright.

This last point is worth making again but in more practical terms. As we pointed out at the beginning of this chapter, the changes in Book of Mormon studies that we're talking about are hard for younger and older alike. And precisely for this reason, far too much that has been published recently about the Book of Mormon has been written in an unnecessarily contentious spirit. This is something that's gone both ways, unfortunately. We feel certain that this contention is among the realest obstacles to Book of Mormon studies going forward. We all have to learn how to get along. All accusing parties ought to become more aware of their tendencies toward defensiveness.

It's essential that there be scholars who write to defend the Book of Mormon against attack. The fact is that many have criticized the Book of Mormon in a mean spirit, dismissively, and with a deliberate aim at offending believers. In the right season and in the right spirit, such criticisms require a response. Others have written about the Book of Mormon in ways that have unintentionally but nonetheless really offended those who believe in its divine authenticity. In the right season, and again in the right spirit, such writers require a bit of correction from believers as well. In short, it's right to defend sacred scripture. This is a duty that Book of Mormon scholars shaped by the twentieth century especially feel, and it is one they execute more consistently than those shaped by the twenty-first century. Those who take up this challenge, though, face a couple of temptations about which they ought to be deeply aware. In defending anything, there's a very real temptation to "return railing for railing" (3 Nephi 6:13), to meet a contentious spirit (or even a perceived contentious spirit) with an equally contentious spirit. This should be avoided. Still more worrisome is a further temptation: to allow defense of the Book of Mormon to become a kind of gatekeeping *among* the Saints. That is, far too often accusations are made by one believer about another. Whether they're written and published or whether they're just whispered into individual ears in quieter settings, such accusations should have no place in the field of Book of Mormon studies. The spirit of accusation slows and stymies Book of Mormon scholarship in tragic ways. It's also at odds with the very spirit of Zion, the community of faith.

Just as much at odds with the spirit of Zion is condescending dismissal of older scholarship by scholars shaped by twenty-first-century concerns. Newer, retooled, and diversifying subdisciplines within Book of Mormon studies are essential to a better understanding of the book. They're important for strictly academic reasons, but they're also important for the work of pressing forward in faith with the founding scripture of the Restoration. Younger members of the Church, certainly in the English-speaking world and often enough beyond it as well, have questions about race, class, gender, violence, war, and exclusion in the Book of Mormon. They need answers they can understand. They *need* them. Further, the Church has become so much more international and diverse in recent decades, and current research projects may do important work in helping the Book of Mormon speak to this much broader body of Saints. It's right to expand the interpretive horizons of the book, and this is something scholars tend to do today. But this comes with its own temptations that require vigilance. It's easy for someone attuned to concerns about race or gender to accuse scholars who sift through the sands of archaeology of political myopia—if not of implicit racism or sexism. It's also easy for someone working in subdisciplines that appeal to scholars outside the community of faith to preen themselves, to be proud of their acceptance in the academy, and so to speak dismissively of scholars who labor to reach believing Latter-day Saints. However, this type of attitude destroys rather than builds Zion. Zion can't be built without, and the Book of Mormon can't shine without, the contributions from all willing scholars of the Book of Mormon.

There's reason, then, to call for a new vocabulary in Book of Mormon studies going forward—the vocabulary that academics refer to when they speak of "charity." To call for charity isn't to call for a dishonestly "nice" way of talking about one another. It certainly isn't to call for eliminating every form of criticism within the community. And it's not to rule out having disagreements or real worries about another's conclusions (even worries that another's conclusions go beyond the boundaries of faithfulness). Instead, a call for charity is a call for us all to recognize our own tendency to misunderstand and misconstrue others. It's a call for us all to have more intellectual humility and to be willing to give one another the benefit of the doubt. In our writing, we display this charity through a slight adjustment of tone. We need a tone that indicates that we're willing to see the best rather than the worst in another's motivations and that invites individuals to clarify positions we may find troubling. Adopting this kind of tone is neither naive nor dishonest, and it's not a way of capitulating to social pressure. It's a way of being honest about how easy it is to misconstrue others' intentions and avoid opportunities to learn.

The writerly generosity we're advocating is particularly important between representatives of different interpretive methods. It's entirely permissible to have strong and deep-seated suspicions about another's approach, but it's wrong and damaging in a myriad of ways to assume without serious and sustained interaction that someone embraces a potentially problematic method only for perverse reasons. For those working within the household of faith, it's far more likely that they do their work with good intentions—that they rightly see something of value that's difficult for another to see or that they wrongly see something of value and stand to learn from generous interaction. And there's nothing to lose in being generous. If we really could learn something from another's approach,

DEFINITION

Academic charity:
The practice of attributing the most reasonable or most defensible argument to one's opponent before critiquing it. In the context of faith, it includes the assumption—unless clear evidence indicates otherwise—that scholars are working in good faith for good purposes.

Overcoming Obstacles

> "And as all have not faith, seek ye diligently and teach one another words of wisdom; yea, seek ye out of the best books words of wisdom; seek learning, even by study and also by faith"
>
> —Doctrine and Covenants 88:118

it would be tragic for us to prohibit friendly discussion. We'd end up only with an impoverished view of the world. And if there really was only error in the other's approach, it would still be tragic for us to have prohibited friendly discussion. We'd end up leaving the other person with an impoverished view of the world, which we might have helped change. Acrimonious debate almost always assumes that it's impossible to learn from each other, but the fact is that there's little that people can learn *without* leaning on each other. Book of Mormon studies will move forward only if it becomes a far friendlier place without compromising anyone's deepest convictions.

Maybe we can put all this another way. In a sense, Book of Mormon studies will flourish the most when it's finally assumed that basically every Latter-day Saint working in the field is doing some kind of faithful apologetics (a term we'll define in a moment). It's disappointingly common to hear Book of Mormon studies talked about as if it were divided between believing apologists and secular scholars, between those who wish to build the kingdom of God and those who wish to build their own careers and reputations. It's just as disappointingly common to hear the same division described as being between those who honestly face up to the real evidence and those who dishonestly defend traditional perspectives. Both sorts of talk are inaccurate. Some scholars, it's true, need to be aware of the lure of following academic trends to establish themselves as intellectual elites. And others, it's true, need to be aware of the enticement of defending whatever is familiar as God's own truth without addressing critical questions. These temptations are real. But the idea that there's a war to be waged among the Saints between believing apologists and secular scholars is simply false. So far, the twenty-first century hasn't witnessed the rise of a faction that resists and sullies apologetics. Rather, what's happened is that *apologetics has been broadened.*

So what is apologetics? Why is it sometimes claimed to be the exclusive property of the faithful? Must it be antagonistic? And why is it sometimes thrown at someone as if it were a bad word, usually coupled with an accusation of conservatism?

The word *apologetics* simply refers to reasoned defense of something, especially something that won't be accepted by everyone. Obviously the truth of the Book of Mormon is something that won't be accepted by everyone. Book of Mormon apologetics is thus simply the reasoned defense of the truth of the Book of Mormon. For the many good reasons that we reviewed in previous chapters, most of the work done on the Book of Mormon in the second half of the twentieth century focused on defending the truth of the Book of Mormon. More specifically, it focused on defending just one dimension of the truth of the Book of Mormon: its claim to be an ancient record. For a long time, Book of Mormon apologetics has been principally—if not in fact exclusively—a practice of defending the ancient historicity of the book. This task has been and remains today an important one for believing Latter-day Saints. To whatever degree it's possible to argue for the Book of Mormon's claims about its antiquity, it ought to be done.

DEFINITION

Apologetics:
Rational defense of traditional faith claims (such as the claim that the Book of Mormon is an ancient book written by inspired prophets).

In light of all this, one way of describing what's happened in recent decades is that many scholars have developed a deeper interest in *other* dimensions of the truth of the Book of Mormon. These other dimensions of the truth of the Book of Mormon do not contradict but add to its ancient historicity. Many people have developed a clear conviction that there's *more* to the truth of the Book of Mormon than has sometimes been assumed. Unfortunately, though, it's sometimes claimed that scholars with a wider range of interests in the truth of the Book of Mormon think there's *less* to the truth of the Book of Mormon than has been assumed in the past. It's sometimes assumed that a particular scholar's interest in other dimensions of the truth of the Book of Mormon is an indication that he or she means to *avoid* the Book of Mormon's antiquity. For the majority of individuals asking new questions or providing new answers in earnest, though, the aim is precisely to *deepen* and *defend* the truth of the Book of Mormon, more broadly conceived. It's to acknowledge the important apologetic work that's already been done and to push that forward.

It's time for all accusation and all questioning of motivation to cease. We can feel confident doing this because taking the Book of Mormon seriously is already assuming the position of the apologist. We need to recognize that both scholars particularly shaped by twentieth-century concerns and scholars particularly shaped by twenty-first-century concerns are all apologists together, to the extent that they work seriously on the Book of Mormon. All earnest readers of the Book of Mormon attune themselves to its truth, even if in the act of thinking further about difficult issues they occasionally draw conclusions that make more traditional believers temporarily uncomfortable. Certainly all readers of the Book of Mormon who explicitly avow faith in the truth of the book deserve the benefit of the doubt from all other readers who avow faith in the truth of the book. We're all working on a truth that's grander than any of our individual approaches to it can reveal.

What we're saying here might seem more obvious after considering how traditional apologists proceed when they work. They don't simply marshal self-interpreting evidence that the Book of Mormon is historical—say, by simply pointing to archaeological discoveries that just *obviously* bolster the Book of Mormon's antiquity. In other words, they aren't simple gatherers of information that's just waiting there for anyone to come along and pick it up. Rather, traditional apologists stop us in our intellectual tracks when they show us that we're overlooking evidence for the Book of Mormon's historicity because we don't read carefully enough. Take the towering figure of Hugh Nibley, for instance. In all his apologetic work on the Book of Mormon, he (1) showed people how to be more sophisticated and discerning readers of the Book of Mormon text, (2) further showed people how to be more open-minded and imaginative readers of ancient history generally, and (3) explained how a discerning reading of the Book of Mormon might allow it to link up with freshly understood ancient history. This is what good traditional apologetics looks like. It leaves neither the Book of Mormon nor ancient history in the state it found them. It transforms both in the name of faith, seeking insight and understanding.

This is exactly what earnest and compelling Book of Mormon scholars are seeking to do today, whether they're working on historical questions or on the many other questions making up the field. An uninteresting study of gender in the Book of Mormon provides only a brief statistical analysis of the book's overt references to women, drawing the apparently obvious conclusion that it's misogynistic. But this isn't what good work on gender in the Book of Mormon has been doing at all. Fascinating recent studies of gender in the Book of Mormon show that there's something going on with women and men in the text that most readers don't see. Effective scholars simultaneously link a sophisticated reading of the text with an imaginative and thoughtful intervention in the field of gender studies. Similarly, a simple study of intertextuality in the Book of Mormon just points out that there's New Testament language in the text and facilely concludes that this means that the King James Bible was among the Book of Mormon's sources. But this isn't what good work on intertextuality has been doing either. Fascinating recent studies on intertextuality in the Book of Mormon show that there's striking and unexpected creativity in the book's handling of New Testament language, working to clarify the nature of textual borrowing and its rhetorical impact on readers.

Thus, in the end, good Book of Mormon scholarship of the new sort proceeds in exactly the way traditional apologists have. The only real difference between earlier forms of scholarship and recent approaches to the Book of Mormon is that there's an effort being made to discover additional dimensions of the book's truth—to turn the interpretive kaleidoscope in the hope of seeing more. In other words, the twenty-first century has marked *not* the slow and agonizing death of Book of Mormon apologetics but rather the dramatic expansion of Book of Mormon apologetics. Elder Neal A. Maxwell once said that he wished to see believing scholars ensure that there were no "uncontested slam dunks" against the Book of Mormon.[2] What motivates newer forms of Book of Mormon scholarship is quite precisely growing recognition that there are games other than that of history where slam dunks are going on—without much of a response. Young readers of the Book of

Mormon are as likely to put the book down over questions about racism, gender, or violence today as they are over questions about historicity. They're as likely to give up on the book because they feel that it doesn't have compelling theology or that it reads as literarily quaint, if not boring, as they are because they have questions about its historicity. In our experience, in fact, they're *more* likely to be concerned about these issues than they are about historicity. New forms of Book of Mormon scholarship are working to provide answers for these readers and their questions. Older forms of Book of Mormon scholarship are necessary to continue to provide answers about familiar questions as well—questions that come up again and again.

Elder Neal A. Maxwell

Now we've argued in this chapter that Book of Mormon scholars should give one another the benefit of the doubt. We've said in this context that it's best to see all earnest participants in Book of Mormon studies as part of the same larger apologetic enterprise. We'd like to add here that it might even be advisable to speak of nonbelievers who try to seriously understand what the Book of Mormon says or how it works as part of the larger apologetic enterprise, at least in a certain regard. When a scholar outside the faith reads the Book of Mormon carefully and honestly, showing believers its depth and richness, shouldn't we welcome them into the conversation with open arms? In our view, such scholars fulfill in an interesting way a passage from Isaiah (one of Nephi's favorites): "Thus saith the Lord God, Behold, I will lift up mine hand to the Gentiles, and set up my standard to the people: and they shall bring thy sons in their arms, and thy daughters shall be carried upon their shoulders. And kings shall be thy nursing fathers, and their queens thy nursing mothers" (Isaiah 49:22–23). Our own precious book is being enriched by the sacrifices and honor not only of our own covenant sisters and brothers—scholars from within the ranks of the believers—but also of those who stand outside our faith. Most Book of Mormon scholars, whether traditional Latter-day Saints or not, are serving today as nursing fathers and nursing mothers, carrying the Book of Mormon in their arms and on their shoulders as they help in the divine work of the book's coming forth.

NOTES

1. See Truman G. Madsen, "B. H. Roberts and the Book of Mormon," *BYU Studies* 19, no. 4 (1979): 427–45; and Matthew Bowman, "Biblical Criticism, the Book of Mormon, and the Meanings of Civilization," *Journal of Book of Mormon Studies* 30 (2021): 62–89.
2. Neal A. Maxwell, quoted in Gilbert W. Scharffs, "I Have a Question," *Ensign*, January 1995, 62.

| CHAPTER 4 |

Common Questions

Part of what characterizes Book of Mormon studies today is developing interest in issues and methods that appeal both to practicing believers who write about the Book of Mormon and to non–Latter-day Saint scholars. So one way to get more precise about what's changing is to look at how scholars working in the last decade or two answer traditional questions in Book of Mormon studies and to contrast their responses with those of their forebears. We've also made the case, though, that part of what distinguishes today's Book of Mormon studies from yesterday's is a broadening of the field and of what "the truth of the Book of Mormon" means. Accordingly, a second way to look more precisely at what's changing is to look directly at newer questions and methods and spell out some of their implications.

We'll dedicate the present chapter to the first of these ways of getting precise about the changing shape of Book of Mormon studies. And then we'll dedicate chapter 5 to the second. Here, then, we want to ask how scholars today tend to answer yesterday's questions. We'll do so by asking two questions. First, how did Book of Mormon scholars in the twentieth century approach certain key issues? And second, how do Book of Mormon scholars working now in the twenty-first century tend to approach the same key issues? We'll ask these questions for each of seven different issues in Book of Mormon studies: the nature of the translation of the text, changes made to the text, supposed modern sources for the Book of Mormon, alleged anachronisms within the text, Isaiah's place in the Book of Mormon, the text's use of New Testament language, and the question of Book of Mormon geography.

HOW WAS THE BOOK OF MORMON TRANSLATED?

In chapter 2 we gave some attention to the question of translation in our discussion of the subdiscipline of studying the textual production of the Book of Mormon. This already familiar issue serves as a helpful introduction to changing approaches even to traditional questions. Joseph Smith's story about gold plates and angelic visits has always been a challenge—or even a scandal—to those outside the faith, especially to the irreligious. This of course hasn't changed with rising academic interest in the Book of Mormon. The simple fact that the angel Moroni took the plates away after their translation is an affront to anyone hoping for an unbiased investigation into the Book of Mormon's truth. Left only with an English text (and its various translations into other languages), how is one to determine the relationship between the Book of Mormon and the ancient origins it claims for itself? We call the book a translation, but what does "translation" mean if the translated text can't be compared to the original? There are questions here for believing Latter-day Saints as well. Is there supposed to be a tight correlation between the English text of the Book of Mormon and the characters inscribed on

> **SEVEN QUESTIONS ABOUT THE BOOK OF MORMON**
>
> - How was the Book of Mormon translated?
> - Why have changes been made to the text of the Book of Mormon?
> - Did the Book of Mormon derive from nineteenth-century texts?
> - What about anachronisms in the Book of Mormon?
> - Does language from Isaiah belong in the Book of Mormon?
> - Does the Book of Mormon depend on the New Testament?
> - Where did the events of the Book of Mormon take place?

the gold plates? What was Joseph Smith's role in providing the English text of the book? Does the Book of Mormon reflect only the voices of its ancient and original authors, or does it also reflect the voice of its modern translator?

As we pointed out in chapter 2, over the course of the twentieth century two contrasting positions emerged among believing Book of Mormon scholars in response to these questions. Both positions developed in response to critics of the Book of Mormon. The earlier and perhaps most common position holds that Joseph Smith was given the words he dictated to his scribes, and so he didn't directly inform the shape or diction of the translation. Today this position is usually called the "tight-control" model. It has been especially endorsed by FARMS scholars and particularly by Royal Skousen in recent years. The other position—first endorsed by B. H. Roberts, but more recently in the literature by Blake T. Ostler and Brant A. Gardner—holds that the Prophet received impressions rather than words and that he then had to decide which words (and perhaps even ideas) to use in giving shape to those impressions. This second position is usually called the "loose-control" model. Tight control arguably makes better sense of existing eyewitness descriptions of the translation process, while loose control seems better able to account for aspects of the text that appear more modern than ancient (but without giving up on the antiquity of the text).

> **TWO CONTRASTING POSITIONS**
>
> Traditional model: tight control
>
> The slowly emerging alternative (from B. H. Roberts through Blake Ostler to Brant Gardner): loose control

The tight- and loose-control models represent extremes. There might of course be tighter or looser models on a sliding scale between the most extreme positions. Middle-ground positions might in fact prove most comfortable to believing scholars, since both extreme positions have some explaining to do. Those who have argued for tight control not only have felt pressure to explain every aspect of the text that looks modern in terms of ancient history but also have felt, at times, a responsibility to explain who exactly gave the translation of the text to Joseph Smith. Thus, tight-control theorists have occasionally speculated about which individual on the other side of the veil provided a translation of the ancient text that then appeared on the seer stones. At the other extreme, those who argue for loose control have felt a need to account for existing eyewitness statements that describe Joseph Smith working with a seer stone and some kind of visual experience. And so loose-control theorists have found themselves speculating about how the mind interacts with a seer stone. Seeking a position between these extremes hasn't proven to be much easier. Those somewhere in the middle have had the unenviable task of determining where the contributions of ancient authors end and where the modern Prophet's contribution begins.

To scholars working outside the Latter-day Saint tradition, of course, this whole debate is moot. Rejecting the idea that Joseph Smith had a prophetic gift and rejecting the existence of an ancient New World Israelite people who created gold plates, such scholars simply assume the Book of Mormon had its origins in the nineteenth century. Thus,

A replica of the gold plates. Photo by Gerrit J. Dirkmaat.

the conversation about how much the Book of Mormon reflects ancient sources or a nineteenth-century American perspective, while intense and of obvious interest to believers, remains insider talk. This debate has been most intense among those individuals involved in traditional debates over Book of Mormon historicity. Believing scholars who are more interested in questions we've mentioned in previous chapters and who work to speak to those within and without the Church often refrain from taking an overt position on this insider debate. They prefer to write simply and exclusively about the English text of the Book of Mormon rather than about the relationship between the English text and the gold plates. They of course believe that Moroni delivered gold plates to Joseph Smith but are unsure how much can constructively be done in trying to prove or disprove the divine origins of the plates. There's plenty of work to do just in trying to understand the text God has given the modern world, regardless of what other work can be done to decide how much the respective environments of original production and ultimate translation shape the text we know. Many believing scholars are now putting their efforts toward answering questions simply about the meaning of the text.

For many of these scholars, we could say that their very methods assume a kind of tight control that they nonetheless feel no responsibility to defend. In other words, many believing scholars assume that what we have in the English Book of Mormon represents what God wants us to have and that the Prophet's primary role was as a transmitter of that text. This, though, doesn't mean for such scholars that the text is wholly foreign to the nineteenth-century context in which it appeared. It means only that they're unconvinced that whatever smacks of the nineteenth century was the Prophet's rather than God's contribution. For our own part, we in fact find devotional comfort in the idea that God wished to ensure that an ancient text would have real relevancy in the context of its latter-day appearance. We marvel at God's love and mercy that is manifested in the words he used as he gave the text to his Prophet "in his own language" and idiom so that the text could be given to the world (Doctrine and Covenants 90:11). With this model, the Book of Mormon as God gave it to Joseph Smith through divine means refuses to remain trapped in the ancient world where it originated. Instead, it makes its

> "To the question 'What was the original language of the Book of Mormon?' the real answer is: It is English! For the English of the Book of Mormon comes by revelation, and no one can go beyond revelation in the search for ultimate sources. Let us, then, rejoice in the text we have and not attempt to reconstruct it in Hebrew or Egyptian so that we can then analyze and translate what we have written!"
>
> —Hugh Nibley, *The Prophetic Book of Mormon*

relevance to the modern world evident in the English text, which is our subject of study.

WHY HAVE CHANGES BEEN MADE TO THE TEXT OF THE BOOK OF MORMON?

As Joseph Smith dictated the Book of Mormon's contents to his scribes, they recorded his dictation on what came to be called the original manuscript. As translation ended and printing began, the Prophet assigned Oliver Cowdery to copy the entirety of the original manuscript, thus creating a printer's manuscript for use in production (while the original was kept safe). Although much of the original manuscript no longer exists (much of it was damaged in storage during the nineteenth century), the fragments that do remain can be compared with the printer's manuscript, and there are interesting differences between the two. Some differences suggest simple errors on the copyist's part, others that Cowdery struggled to read the original, and still others that there were transcription errors in the original that needed correcting. We can tell, then, that even before the Book of Mormon saw its way into print, there were already minor difficulties in deciding on the exact text of the book.

Then four editions of the Book of Mormon appeared during Joseph Smith's lifetime, all under his authority but three under his close supervision. The first appeared in 1830 in Palmyra, New York, set by John

Gilbert largely (but not entirely) from the printer's manuscript. Gilbert introduced punctuation along with—occasionally by mistake but at times intentionally—other variants into the text. The second edition appeared in Kirtland, Ohio, in 1837, set anew from the same printer's manuscript. Oliver Cowdery had primary responsibility for printing this edition, but not before Joseph himself directly revised the printer's manuscript with his own pen. The Prophet made over a thousand changes, most of them linked to fixing grammar or updating archaic language. A few changes were of potentially greater significance, however, such as changing "God" to "Son of God" in 1 Nephi 11:18. The Church then issued a third edition of the Book of Mormon in 1840 in Nauvoo, Illinois, with Don Carlos Smith (the Prophet's brother) and Ebenezer Robinson as the printers. This edition included further corrections and a few clarifications, such as a shift from "a white and a delightsome people" to "a pure and a delightsome people" in 2 Nephi 30:6. The printers clearly consulted the original (and not just the printer's) manuscript for this edition and corrected certain errors from the first two editions. Finally, a fourth edition appeared in 1841, removed from Joseph's close supervision because it was published in Liverpool, England. It was largely reproduced from the 1837 edition.

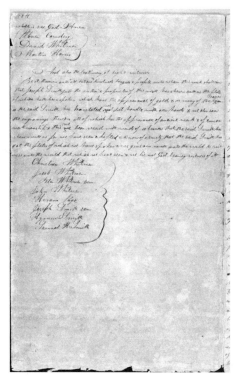

List of Eight Witnesses, Book of Mormon printer's manuscript. Copied by Oliver Cowdery, Church History Library.

The question for believing readers of the Book of Mormon in all this is how to understand the Prophet's consistent efforts to revise the text of the book. If the words of the Book of Mormon were granted by the gift and power of God and correctly written down by scribes, isn't the earliest or original text what God wants us to have in the book? Why change it? And what of the Prophet's famous statement that the Book of Mormon is the most correct of any book?[1] It's true that the overwhelming majority of the changes made by Joseph had to do with grammar, but one might still ask why God wouldn't have given a grammatically flawless text in the first place. Isn't it especially concerning that some changes appear to alter doctrinal content?

These questions occurred to—or were forcefully posed for—Latter-day Saints in the twentieth century as well. Scurrilous pamphlets announcing thousands of changes to a supposedly divine text have appeared occasionally. But sincere questions about the print history of the text have occurred to earnest believers as well. As such, various writers have attempted for a long time to provide answers to questions about the text's transmission history. Really, the full scope of what needs addressing wasn't available to scholars until Royal Skousen's work on the textual history of the Book of Mormon matured. Even before that maturation, though, standard answers took shape that remain in circulation today.

For the most part, what has shaped these answers has been whether the one providing an answer endorses what we now call tight or loose control in understanding the process of translation. For those who embrace loose control—or who at least aren't uncomfortable with a certain degree of looseness in God's control over transcription and publication—the questions are largely toothless. That is, the questions seem to such individuals to have force only if one grants the specific notion that neither ancient nor modern prophets could have been under divine influence while producing grammatically incorrect or theologically imprecise language—things that would require correction or clarification later. A loose-control model rejects this idea at the theoretical level. Those who embrace tight control or push toward the tighter end of the spectrum have tended to come up with other (and sometimes rather ingenious) explanations for the grammar of the Book of Mormon. For example, Royal Skousen and Stanford Carmack have argued that there *is* no incorrect grammar in the Book of Mormon in its earliest form. There's only *nonstandard* grammar, akin to the language of early modern English (from a couple of centuries before Joseph Smith's own nineteenth century).[2] Joseph Smith's and others' editing of the text later was, for such scholars, a human affair—expressions of a sense of propriety had by those who work to see the Book of Mormon received well by its readers.

Many scholars working in the field today tend to regard the changes made to the text of the Book of Mormon as simply a familiar dimension of Joseph Smith's work with his revelations and translations. In this context, we should all recognize that the editorial treatment of the Book of Mormon's text from the moment of its initial reception has been *extremely* conservative. Quick comparisons with the histories of the revelation in the Doctrine and Covenants or the texts making up the so-called Joseph Smith Translation show just how stable the Book of Mormon text has been from the beginning. For many Book of Mormon scholars today, then, the historical changes made to the text of the Book of Mormon are so relatively insignificant and so theologically unimportant that they're largely beside the point. Work on the textual history is of course important, as we discussed at length in a previous chapter, because it enables the best readings of the text. However, from the point of view of most scholars working in the field today, it's only understandable that Joseph Smith received the text in the language and diction that made it immediately accessible to him and those around him and that he and other Church leaders later worked to make it immediately accessible to a wider readership or later generations with more education. The tension in the Book of Mormon's editorial history has always been between modernizing or clarifying the text and leaving the historical and theological teachings of the book untouched. For most today, it looks like the Prophet and his heirs did good and certainly understandable work as they sought to balance competing loyalties.

DID THE BOOK OF MORMON DERIVE FROM NINETEENTH-CENTURY TEXTS?

Once the Book of Mormon was in print, it attracted the attention of critics, and that situation hasn't abated in the nearly two hundred years since it began. One consistent form of critique has been to argue that Joseph Smith was influenced by contemporary texts. Some claimed early on that the so-called Solomon Spaulding manuscript provided a narrative framework the Prophet could easily have adopted. Later it was Ethan Smith's *View of the Hebrews* that some claimed offered Joseph Smith ideas about connections between Israelites and Native American origins. Most recently, Gilbert Hunt's *The Late War between the United States and Great Britain* has been identified as a possible catalyst for Joseph Smith's writing an American history in biblical language. The first of these three alleged influences on the Book of Mormon drew extensive attention in the nineteenth century. The second drew much attention in the twentieth century. The third has only begun to draw attention in the twenty-first century.

Manuscript Found: The Complete Original "Spaulding Manuscript"

The earliest of these three theories asserted that Joseph Smith plagiarized the Book of Mormon from a manuscript written by Solomon Spaulding and passed to Joseph by Sidney Rigdon (who supposedly acquired the manuscript in Pittsburgh, Pennsylvania). Like the Book of Mormon, Spaulding's tale centered on a group of refugees (Roman in Spaulding's story) who landed in the Americas and interacted with different native tribes. Although no one could locate a copy of Spaulding's manuscript, several individuals swore affidavits that the Spaulding manuscript and the Book of Mormon overlapped in several places—including names of characters and major plot points. In 1884, though, Spaulding's actual manuscript resurfaced and made clear that, except at the broadest and therefore irrelevant level, the two manuscripts shared nothing. Apart from a few hobbyists, critics soon ceased to espouse the theory. At about the same time, though, critics turned to *View of the Hebrews* as a possible source text and developed a second theory. In 1823, Ethan Smith, a Congregationalist pastor from Vermont, published a well-received book arguing that Native Americans descended from the lost tribes of Israel. Parallels between *View of the Hebrews* and the Book of Mormon were more compelling than those between Spaulding's manuscript and the Book of Mormon. B. H. Roberts, a believing Church leader in the first half of the twentieth century, famously wrestled long and perhaps inconclusively with parallels he found between the two books. Even in this case, though, the parallels are too broad to justify any theory of actual dependence, and the differences in conception are striking and important.

A newer theory, motivated in a similar way, has emerged in just the last few years. *The Late War* plays the key role in the most recent attempt to discover a secular source for the Book of Mormon. This book, written in 1816 by Gilbert J. Hunt, was an attempt at a history of the War of 1812 in biblical style, representative of a genre of "pseudo-biblical" histories popular in the United States around the beginning of the nineteenth century. Because the book uses phrases such as "and it came to pass," alludes to "freemen" and "king-men," includes a possible chiasm, narrates the building of a ship, and relays a story of two thousand soldiers who fight against King George III, some have argued that Joseph Smith read *The Late War* in school and (consciously or even unconsciously) modeled the Book of Mormon after it. As with *View of the Hebrews*, many of the parallels in this case are broad or general ones, and similarities in language are rooted in both books having a biblical style (that of the King James Version).

View of the Hebrews

Unsurprisingly, Latter-day Saint scholars have worked throughout the history of the Church to discredit these theories. While the Spaulding theory eventually undid itself (with even a critical biographer like Fawn M. Brodie emphatically refuting it), the Book of Mormon's possible connections with *View of the Hebrews* and *The Late War* are still objects of interest today. For the most part, responses to these latter two theories have taken the shape of careful articulations of the real and telling differences between the alleged sources and the Book of Mormon itself. Establishing actual literary dependence is very difficult, especially the direct literary dependence that would be needed for a compellingly definitive argument against the Book of Mormon's antiquity. At most, similarities between the Book of Mormon and *View of the Hebrews* or *The Late War* suggest that certain biblically influenced ideas and certain biblical turns of phrase were in the air in the early nineteenth century. But that's no surprise. That the Book of Mormon would show up in a context where it would make cultural sense is the kind of thing any believer in the book ought to affirm.

For precisely these reasons, many or most scholars working in the field of Book of Mormon studies today don't give much time or attention to these tired theories about alleged nineteenth-century sources for the Book of Mormon. Of course, some scholars working in the field do pay attention to these works, but principally as resources for clarifying the cultural context in which the Book of Mormon appeared and within which it had its first impact. Even non–Latter-day Saint scholars like Elizabeth Fenton (writing about Ethan Smith) and Eran Shalev (writing about Gilbert Hunt) don't express interest in questions about the Book of Mormon's sources but rather in questions about how the Book of Mormon was received in a context where books like *View of the Hebrews* and *The Late War* were popular. Thus, while understanding why potential connections between these works and the Book of Mormon might be troubling to believers, Book of Mormon scholars today tend to turn to these works with a completely different set of questions—hoping mostly to understand where and how the Book of Mormon was unique and where and how it may have changed popular understandings of the location of the lost ten tribes of Israel or the usefulness of biblical language in presenting history.

WHAT ABOUT ANACHRONISMS IN THE BOOK OF MORMON?

Other long-standing critiques of the Book of Mormon concern elements of the text that might seem to fit better into the nineteenth-century context of the book's appearance than in the ancient world. We briefly mentioned such elements above in connection with theories of translation. Still other long-standing critiques focus on things mentioned in the book that someone like Joseph Smith might have naturally believed would fit but that wouldn't fit in pre-Columbian America, according to the best of current scientific knowledge. These sorts of critiques thus concern anachronisms—that is, things out of place in the time that the text claims to describe. Critics, for instance, point to the Book of Mormon's references to steel and silk or to horses and elephants. Or they point to things like (relatively) democratic ideas or ideals, strongly racializing language, or religious questions of particular concern in pre–Civil War American culture. For critics, these kinds of things suggest origins in the nineteenth century. For believers, some explanation is needed. Unfortunately, these details are harder to explain than any of the supposed problems we've surveyed in the previous three sections.

> **DEFINITION**
>
> *Anachronism:*
> A detail in a text that doesn't appear to fit in the historical period in which the text is set or is supposed to have been created.

The kinds of responses to these difficulties from early in the history of the Church and continuing into the late twentieth century aren't hard to imagine. Some have pointed out the fallibility of archaeology as a discipline or underscored its being in an infant state for ancient America. Some have pointed to certain obstacles to archaeology in particular regions where the Book of Mormon's events may have taken place, or they point to scattered anomalies in the archaeological record that suggest a more complicated picture than the current consensus endorses. Some have explored the possibility that certain English words in the Book of Mormon are approximations for ancient words that shouldn't be taken too literally or that they're accurately translated but were brought by Jaredites, Nephites, or Lamanites from the Old World and then used (technically inaccurately) to refer to somewhat similar New World things. Others point out sometimes subtle and sometimes not-so-subtle differences between political ideas or religious issues as they're raised in the Book of Mormon and as they were of concern in nineteenth-century America. In most such work, the emphasis has been on explaining away each potential anachronism, one by one.

For many scholars working in the context of twenty-first-century Book of Mormon studies, though, it seems these difficulties don't hold their attention often or for long. Those who have written on the issue (for example, Adam S. Miller) tend to point out that anachronisms are something one should naturally expect from any good or useful translation.

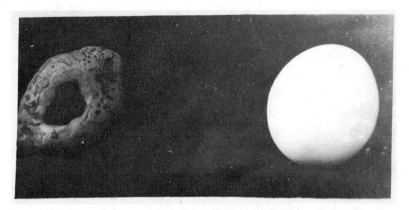

Image of green seer stone next to an egg. Courtesy of L. Tom Perry Special Collections, Harold B. Lee Library, Brigham Young University.

The Book of Mormon, after all, claims only that it's a translation, by the gift and power of God, of what was written anciently by a few men whose eyes were squarely and prophetically focused on the last days. And prophecy is itself anachronistic—out of sync with the time of its utterance. So also is translation an anachronistic enterprise, a representation of things native to one context featured in a wholly different context, alienated from its proper time as it inhabits another. If the Book of Mormon weren't anachronistic in certain ways, it would be unintelligible to modern readers. Also, if it weren't anachronistic in a deep sense, it wouldn't be prophetic or prepared to call the world to repentance in the last days.[3] Of course, this or that particular anachronism might well get under someone's skin, and there's certainly reason to work up some explanation of it. For many today, though, what's most important about addressing any particular anachronism in the Book of Mormon is to *understand* the passage or context in which it appears. Indeed, for the believer, to see this task as important is itself a gesture of faith. And where it isn't immediately possible to answer all the questions we have about the text, believing scholars seem to trust that it's occasionally necessary to sit patiently and faithfully, living with a bit of mystery and refusing to let lingering concerns distract them from what matters most.

Common Questions

DOES ISAIAH BELONG IN THE BOOK OF MORMON?

> **PREVAILING VIEWS OF ISAIAH AUTHORSHIP**
>
> Mainstream biblical scholarship divides Isaiah into three parts:
>
> - First Isaiah (chapters 1–39), with origins in the eighth century before Christ, tied to Isaiah of Jerusalem
> - Second Isaiah (chapters 40–55), with origins allegedly in the sixth century before Christ, tied to an unnamed prophet in either Babylon or Palestine
> - Third Isaiah (chapters 56–66), with origins late in the sixth century or early in the fifth century before Christ, tied to an unnamed prophet in Jerusalem

Two potential anachronisms in the Book of Mormon deserve more discussion because they have drawn a special sort of attention in past literature and in present research. The first concerns Isaiah. The past century and a half has seen a consensus emerge among biblical scholars that the book of Isaiah weaves together writings that originated in three dramatically different periods of Israel's history. The first set of writings is generally believed to go back to Isaiah of Jerusalem, who wrote during the eighth century before Christ. The second and third sets of writings, however, are believed to have originated more than a century later than Isaiah's own lifetime and to have been appended to the collection of Isaiah's writings long after his death. Isaiah scholars debate the details, but the vast majority agree on the general picture. It's important to note that there are Isaiah scholars who take a dissenting position, but nearly all who dissent begin from conservative Christian theological assumptions about biblical inerrancy (that is, the idea that the Bible is wholly without error because it's God's word).

All this poses difficulties for the Book of Mormon because Nephi (and Abinadi more briefly) quotes from certain supposedly later portions of the book of Isaiah. According to the Book of Mormon, Nephi and his family left Jerusalem with the brass plates (Nephi's source for Isaiah) at the beginning of the sixth century before Christ. At least parts of what he quotes from Isaiah, however, are generally believed to have originated no earlier than a few decades into the sixth century—and certain other parts still later. Even the uncontested parts of Isaiah that

The Great Isaiah Scroll. Courtesy of Wikimedia Commons.

Nephi quotes, it's often argued, only received the shape they have in the Book of Mormon rather late, decades after Nephi's family would have left for the promised land. The predominant scholarly consensus thus suggests that there's something anachronistic about the Book of Mormon's quotations of Isaiah. Put simply, to some it seems Nephi quoted from a text that didn't yet exist at the time he was writing his record. This difficulty has long been recognized by Latter-day Saint scholars, who have been writing about it since the 1930s.

Too eager to solve this potential problem for the Book of Mormon quickly, some have suggested that biblical scholars come to their conclusions simply because they don't believe in real (predictive) prophecy. In other words, they don't believe that Isaiah could have been aware of events that would occur after his lifetime and thus believe that he could not have written about them. But this response, which already appeared in the 1930s, unfortunately oversimplifies matters. It's true that biblical scholars—and really, scholars of all kinds—are too quick to draw secu-

---

PARTS OF ISAIAH QUOTED IN THE BOOK OF MORMON THAT MAINSTREAM BIBLICAL SCHOLARS WOULD OBJECT TO

- Isaiah 48–49 (in 1 Nephi 20–21)
- Isaiah 50–51 (in 2 Nephi 7–8)
- Scattered passages in Isaiah 2–14; 29 (in 2 Nephi 12–24; 27)
- Isaiah 52 (in Mosiah 12; 3 Nephi 20)
- Isaiah 53 (in Mosiah 15)
- Isaiah 54 (in 3 Nephi 22)

larizing conclusions without having sifted all the evidence, but there are various kinds of evidence that have led scholars to their conclusions regarding Isaiah's authorship. Additionally, it's uncharitable and inaccurate to insist that the conclusions of biblical scholarship result solely or even primarily from the scholars' worldviews. To be sure, worldviews always play a role in scholarship, but so does evidence, and it's the evidence that needs to be dealt with. To show that passages from the book of Isaiah quoted in the Book of Mormon existed in their final form by the time Nephi acquired the brass plates, it would be necessary to engage directly and convincingly with the evidence for dating discussed by Isaiah scholars. Notably, more substantial responses along such lines did indeed appear at various points in the twentieth century. Such work most commonly investigated the places where the Book of Mormon's version of Isaiah's words differs from the biblical version. Scholars from Sidney B. Sperry to John A. Tvedtnes labored to show that some of these variants match up with other variant Isaiah texts known from the ancient world in unanticipated and surprising ways.[4]

In many ways, though, the question of whether the Book of Mormon's uses of Isaiah are decidedly anachronistic hasn't yet been asked earnestly. It isn't enough for critics to point to scholarly consensus to establish that the Book of Mormon stumbles on this point. Consensus changes, and it always has blind spots. But it also isn't enough for defenders of the Book of Mormon's antiquity to line up scattered points of evidence regarding the single authorship of Isaiah or to cast aspersions on the motivations of biblical scholars. The fact is that no Isaiah scholar has yet fully tested the hypothesis that all the parts of

Isaiah quoted in the Book of Mormon (and no more) had their final form by the beginning of the sixth century before Christ. Non–Latter-day Saint scholars frankly have no motivation to pursue this hypothesis, and Latter-day Saint scholars with relevant training haven't given sufficient attention directly to this question to decide it compellingly. Nothing definitive—certainly nothing definitive enough to risk one's faith commitments on—has yet appeared in answer to such questions. It would be wonderful to see this issue receive the most serious treatment possible. For the moment, that hasn't happened, and so every conclusion drawn is premature.

Further, though, it's simply unclear just how important it would actually be to show that every Isaiah passage quoted in the Book of Mormon had been authored and given final shape by Nephi's day. Grant Hardy—representative of the perspective of many twenty-first-century Book of Mormon scholars—has suggested that God might simply have wished for modern readers of the Book of Mormon to have a fuller Isaiah text than was available to Nephi on the brass plates. Because we don't have access to the gold plates that the Book of Mormon was translated from, or to the brass plates that Nephi asserts to have drawn his Isaiah text from, we don't know how exactly the English text of the Book of Mormon is meant to reproduce the ancient sources. For many of today's Book of Mormon scholars, then, it seems much too hasty for a believer to decide against the Book of Mormon's truth because of its uses of Isaiah. And precisely for this reason, study of Isaiah in the Book of Mormon in recent scholarship has taken a decidedly different tack than work in the twentieth century. Rather than working to decide whether the Book of Mormon is or isn't historically defensible in including Isaiah passages, they work to ask just what role the book of Isaiah plays in the Book of Mormon. What do Isaiah texts add to the book's message? How do they shape it or its theological perspective? Scholars asking these questions have begun to show that Isaiah is far more important to the Book of Mormon than has often been assumed and that the Book of Mormon has a consequent theological depth that's been overlooked in certain ways.

DOES LANGUAGE FROM THE NEW TESTAMENT BELONG IN THE BOOK OF MORMON?

A second potential anachronism worthy of special note is the Book of Mormon's use of language reminiscent of the King James New Testament. New Testament language is, in fact, substantially more present in the text than is often recognized. Some have suggested that this is a threat to the Book of Mormon's historicity—with Mark Twain already in the nineteenth century calling the Book of Mormon a plagiarism of the King James Bible.[5] The question has some force: How could a book with origins in a 600 BC migration from Jerusalem to the Americas contain passages from the standard nineteenth-century English translation of the New Testament? Phrases from (at least parts of) the Old Testament might well be expected, since the Nephites possessed some version of writings known in the Old Testament. But the presence of language from, say, the Gospel of John in 1 Nephi 10 is more difficult to understand, as the Gospel of John (not to mention every other book of the New Testament) wouldn't have been written until centuries after Nephi's death. Naturally, as with all criticisms of Book of Mormon historicity, there are various ways this issue has been dealt with.

The earliest and still the most traditional approach was to argue (or simply to assume, as the earliest Saints seemed to do) that New Testament language appears in the Book of Mormon because that's what was inscribed on the gold plates by the book's inspired ancient authors. With this view, the Book of Mormon is not directly dependent on the New Testament. The two have similar language, it's true, but only because God reveals the same things to all peoples and at all times. A slight variation on this view eventually emerged, however. This was the idea that the ancient authors of the Book of Mormon were given, through divine experiences, knowledge of the language of the New Testament itself in advance, and so they used it in their writings. Nephite prophets in fact occasionally explain that they saw the last days and had a message directly intended for those living in a late Christian context. Yet another variation began to appear in the 1940s and 1950s that has proven quite enduring. This was the idea that Book of Mormon authors and New Testament authors had access to similarly worded ancient texts (in, say, the brass plates) that aren't extant today.

Such shared sources would contain older textual traditions that played a role in the composition of the Book of Mormon (such as Moroni 7) but also of parts of the New Testament (such as 1 Corinthians 13). What united all these early and enduring approaches from the beginning was an implicit tight-control model of translation. They all, in other words, took the text to be a word-for-word translation of the gold plates, which already had what we'd today recognize as New Testament language in them.

Another set of approaches has gained ascendancy in recent years, in large part owing to the emergence and popularization of the loose-control model of translation. These more recent approaches have also insisted on the existence of ancient gold plates and some correlation between the plates and the English text of the Book of Mormon. They have also, though, acknowledged that because any translator has to make choices about how to best make one language resonate in another, the English text might be expected to take certain liberties with the underlying gold-plates text. That is, these more recent approaches have taken the Book of Mormon's English text as introducing New Testament language into an ancient text that wasn't originally worded that way. Some among this school of thought have understood a looser translation like this to be the product of Joseph Smith's own involvement, whether larger or smaller, in producing the English text. Others have taken it to be the work of some divine being—God or an angel—before the English words' appearance on the seer stone. Either way, those who have embraced a looser notion of translation have tended to see a variety of reasons for a less literal translation.

DEFINITION

Rhetorical authority: Refers to the credibility granted a text based on its relationship to established authoritative sources. For example, the Book of Mormon exhibits its status as scripture through the presence of New Testament language in it, since the Bible was the principal source of cultural authority for readers in the nineteenth century.

New Testament language makes the Book of Mormon more intelligible to a latter-day (and largely Christian) audience. It also lends rhetorical authority to the Book of Mormon, allowing it to speak in the voice of authoritative scripture.

Just as many believing scholars contributing to Book of Mormon studies today feel it unnecessary to take sides in the late twentieth-century and early twenty-first-century debate over tight and loose control, many of them do not seem to have strong feelings about just how or why New Testament language found its way into the English text of the Book of Mormon. Many take it for granted that the language is there and seek instead to ask what role such language plays in giving the text meaning. Happy to grant that the language is there by God's design—however he made it happen—they ask questions like the following: Does the Book of Mormon simply reproduce New Testament tropes and turns of phrase, or does it recast New Testament language in theologically interesting ways? Do certain Book of Mormon figures share language with certain New Testament writers or figures, and is that significant? How does the use of the language of a specific New Testament author change over the course of the Book of Mormon, and what might that imply theologically? In pursuing these kinds of questions, Book of Mormon scholars today are beginning to discern a much more theologically robust and compelling picture that went unseen while the dominant question asked was whether New Testament language is a liability for the Book of Mormon.

WHERE DID THE EVENTS OF THE BOOK OF MORMON TAKE PLACE?

Perhaps no topic is more hotly debated among amateur Book of Mormon enthusiasts today than that of geography. It might even be said that no topic has been more popular among amateur Book of Mormon enthusiasts since the book's initial publication than questions of geography and archaeology. While there have been different theories as to where Book of Mormon events exactly took place, one model in particular became by far the most popular by the middle of the twentieth century, only gaining prominence as the century wore on. This model has suggestively placed Book of Mormon events in a limited geographic area somewhere in Central America (most popularly in the Tehuantepec region of southern Mexico and Guatemala). What gave rise to this Mesoamerican model was the presence in the region of developed urban areas during the last few centuries before Christ, as well as stronger geographic correlation to features mentioned in the Book of Mormon. It certainly helped that the 1950s saw (thanks to M. Wells Jakeman) the popularization of the idea that a monumental stela (an upright decorated stone slab) from this area was connected directly to Lehi's famous dream in 1 Nephi 8. When John L. Sorenson succeeded Jakeman as the chief Book of Mormon geographer in the 1980s and 1990s, he (along with others) made a strikingly sustained case for the Mesoamerican model, even garnering implicit Church support by publishing some of his findings in the Church's *Ensign* magazine. In the twenty-first century, Sorenson's work has been furthered in important ways by Brant A. Gardner, Mark Alan Wright, and Kerry M. Hull.

The Mesoamerican model arose in major part as a complex and positive response to general skepticism about whether Nephite and Lamanite ruins could be found in America in any identifiable way. Correlations and correspondences suggested that skeptics entertained doubts about the viability of Book of Mormon archaeology too hastily. And when scholars like Sorenson occasionally drew impressive concessions from established scholars outside the faith, such as Cyrus H. Gordon, it certainly seemed that a Mesoamerican setting for the Book of Mormon might make the volume's historicity intellectually defensible. From the beginning there were, of course, difficulties that the Mesoamerican model had to deal with. Those who endorsed the model quickly developed explanations and responses to these anomalies, however. A good example concerned simply the enormous geographic distance between Mesoamerica and the New York hill where Joseph Smith found the gold plates by angelic direction. In response to this issue, Mesoamerican scholars have argued that the Hill Cumorah spoken about in the Book of Mormon is a hill somewhere in Mesoamerica rather than the hill in New York that was the plates' final resting place. Moroni, they've pointed out, journeyed for literal decades after the war at Cumorah and may have wandered quite far from where the Nephites were annihilated. (This is sometimes called the "two-Cumorah" theory.)

In recent years, the dominance of the Mesoamerican model has come into question. Among trained scholars, it has retained solid and even majority support. Among lay enthusiasts, however, other models

Photograph of the Hill Cumorah taken in 1907. Courtesy of Wikimedia Commons.

for Book of Mormon geography have emerged, one of them with an astonishing level of support among American Latter-day Saints. This last is what's been dubbed the Heartland model of Book of Mormon geography. Those who espouse the Heartland model have passionately argued that all the events of the Book of Mormon took place in North America, specifically within the boundaries of the United States. Under this model, the Hill Cumorah of the text is in fact in New York, the River Sidon is the Mississippi River, and the west sea is one of the Great Lakes. Although some questionable archaeological data has appeared in writings endorsing this model, most of the evidence for it has derived from statements made by early Church leaders, such as a letter written by Oliver Cowdery and published in an early Church newspaper (the so-called Letter VII).[6] What ultimately seem to have been the primary motivations for the rise of the Heartland model, however, are political motivations—and in particular an idea of American exceptionalism. One motivation for this idea seems to be that Book of Mormon events

> "The Church does not take a position on the specific geographic locations of Book of Mormon events in the ancient Americas. Speculation on the geography of the Book of Mormon may mislead instead of enlighten; such a study can be a distraction from its divine purpose."
>
> —Gospel Topics, "Book of Mormon Geography," topics.ChurchofJesusChrist.org

occurred within the boundaries of the modern United States because the United States as a Christian nation is divinely ordained.

As the intensity of online and otherwise published debate over Book of Mormon geography has grown—alongside a lack of definitive archaeological evidence to decide among the options—Church leadership has increasingly taken a neutral position.[7] Likewise, most Book of Mormon scholars working in recent years have taken a neutral position. Although a few trained scholars continue to work in serious and interesting ways on connecting the Book of Mormon directly to its possible ancient American settings, the majority turn their attention elsewhere, leaving questions of geography to a few specialists and a large body of amateurs. For most, it seems, locating a geographic setting that might definitively inform interpretation of the text will become possible only with more definite information or undeniable archaeological finds. Until then, for such scholars, it seems best to give scholarly attention to dramatically understudied aspects of the text. Even among those scholars who do give serious attention to the Book of Mormon's ancient American setting (Kerry M. Hull is a particularly good example), it's become common to entertain a variety of possible settings in the ancient Americas in order to let archaeological research inform an interpretation of the text.

* * *

Even the cursory survey above reveals what those working in Book of Mormon studies have known for a long time: that real intellectual challenges face the believing scholar who wishes to leave no question unanswered. The Saints have had their good reasons to believe what they have claimed about the book, but those who oppose these claims have provided their own honest reasons for doing so. Precisely for this reason, Latter-day Saint scholars have long labored to defend the truth of the Book of Mormon—both its spiritual and its historical truth. At the same time, in part because Book of Mormon studies has begun to grow into a field of study in its own right and in part because of larger changes in the intellectual climate, traditional challenges to the Book of Mormon play a less dominant role in Book of Mormon studies today than they have in the past. Other questions have risen into prominence, and these are questions that need serious responses. Answering these other questions has in turn helped to shape new answers to the older questions as well. For anyone hoping to defend the place the Book of Mormon might occupy in the twenty-first century as a volume of scripture that demands believing adherents, familiarity with and sympathy toward new and changing questions are crucial. Taking such questions seriously today—like taking traditional questions seriously yesterday and today—is not a gesture of doubt but rather a demonstration of faith. It's to trust that the Book of Mormon can hold up against our best scrutiny.

NOTES

1. See Joseph Smith, History, 1838–1856, volume C-1 [2 November 1838–31 July 1842], p. 1255, *The Joseph Smith Papers*, https://www.josephsmithpapers.org/paper-summary/history-1838-1856-volume-c-1-2-november-1838-31-july-1842/427.
2. See Royal Skousen, with the collaboration of Stanford Carmack, *The History of the Text of the Book of Mormon, Volume 3, Part 1: Grammatical Variation* (Provo, UT: BYU Studies, 2016), 3–95.
3. See, for instance, Adam S. Miller, "Messianic History: Walter Benjamin and the Book of Mormon," in *Rube Goldberg Machines: Essays in Mormon Theology* (Salt Lake City: Greg Kofford Books, 2012), 21–35.
4. See Sidney B. Sperry, *Our Book of Mormon* (Salt Lake City: Bookcraft, 1947), 172–77; and John A. Tvedtnes, *The Isaiah Variants in the Book of Mormon* (Provo, UT: FARMS, 1981).
5. See Mark Twain, *Roughing It* (New York: Harper and Brothers, 1913), 1:110.
6. For this letter, see Oliver Cowdery, "Letter VII," *Latter Day Saints' Messenger and Advocate*, July 1835, 155–59.
7. See Gospel Topics, "Book of Mormon Geography," topics.ChurchofJesusChrist.org.

| CHAPTER 5 |

New Directions

In the preceding chapter, we looked at traditional issues in Book of Mormon studies, comparing twentieth-century approaches to these issues with responses to them discernable in the work of twenty-first-century scholars. Today, two decades into the twenty-first century, there are many active researchers still working on these issues. Some of these, despite developments in the field, continue to work on either questioning or bolstering the Book of Mormon's claim to being an ancient book. As we've said, however, fewer well-trained researchers work in traditional ways on such problems today than just a few years ago. Most of these issues, as we've detailed in chapter 4, play a different role in the hands of today's students of the Book of Mormon. In this final chapter, we want to look at the new questions and methods that have arisen in the twenty-first century, largely positioned beyond the questions and concerns of twentieth-century Book of Mormon studies.

Before we do so, however, it's worth pausing to think about whether there's something problematic about the shifts we detailed in the preceding chapter. As laudable as it may sound to say that Book of Mormon scholars today are working productively and amicably with academics positioned outside the faith tradition, aren't there legitimate worries about treating the Book of Mormon in a way that allows it to become a neutral object of investigation? Shouldn't the Book of Mormon *always* be controversial, a scandal of sorts, provoking outsiders enough that they ask the question of whether the book is true? Might Book of Mormon studies in its newest forms be watering the Book of Mormon's message down so that it's more palatable to nonbelievers, ultimately secularizing the sacred? We argued in chapter 3 that scholars shaped by late twentieth-century Book of Mormon studies and scholars shaped by early twenty-first-century Book of Mormon studies ought to learn from one another. But might it simply be the case that more recent developments actually *do* mark a departure from the faith in some way? The fact is that the sketches in chapter 4 need some defense and justification. Before we go any further in describing what's changed in Book of Mormon studies, we have to ask *whether* Book of Mormon studies ought to move in the directions it has recently.

The questions in the last paragraph all point in the same direction. They all suggest, to one degree or another, that Book of Mormon scholarship would become more palatable to outsiders only by design—that is, because Book of Mormon scholars decide one day to *make* the Book of Mormon palatable to outsiders. The questions also imply that Book of Mormon scholarship could only go in the direction it's been going in order to *capitulate* to some force felt from outside the faith. And so, some fear that all the talk in chapter 3 about a broadened conception of what it means to speak of the truth of the Book of Mormon may really be a fancy and seductive way of saying that we ought to redefine truth—perhaps in a postmodern fashion—so as to get along with the sophisticated and the secular. This, however, is entirely false. Rather, there are deeply *religious* and wholly *nonsecular* motivations that have driven the broadening and redirection of Book of Mormon studies in recent years, and newer work has simply had as one of its incidental (but very welcome) byproducts a certain reception in the larger scholarly world.

Part of what's driven changes in Book of Mormon studies is what Terryl L. Givens explained in *By the Hand of Mormon: The American Scripture That Launched a New World Religion*, as we've talked about before. That is, much of the work done on both sides of the question of historicity—work done by critics of and work done by defenders of

> "Let us take the Book of Mormon, which a man took and hid in his field, securing it by his faith, to spring up in the last days, or in due time; let us behold it coming forth out of the ground, which is indeed accounted the least of all seeds, but behold it branching forth, yea, even towering, with lofty branches, and God-like majesty, until it, like the mustard seed, becomes the greatest of all herbs."
>
> —Joseph Smith, "Letter to the Elders of the Church, 30 November–1 December 1835," *The Joseph Papers*

the Book of Mormon's antiquity—seems to be in a relatively finished state. There's seldom much that's new these days in the battle over the Book of Mormon's historicity. Critics today tend to retread the ground of their forebears without adding any substantially new arguments or evidence. For the most part, they tend just to update the rhetoric or the distribution platforms of those who have criticized Book of Mormon historicity before them, hoping to reach newer or younger audiences. Like the critics, defenders today tend to retread the ground of their own scholarly forebears while adding few substantially new arguments or evidence. They also, in other words, mostly tend to update the rhetoric or the distribution platforms of those who have defended the Book of Mormon before them. Defenders of the Book of Mormon's historicity have in particular worked tirelessly to make their work accessible to younger Latter-day Saints through the use of new media, including social media. Exemplary in this regard are those who work at Book of Mormon Central. They labor to ensure that robust intellectual defenses of the Book of Mormon worked out by past generations are immediately discoverable by those who encounter traditional criticisms of the Book of Mormon for the first time.

We should of course keep our eyes peeled for updates and developments on the traditional question of Book of Mormon historicity—emerging new angles, pressing new questions that require careful answers, or more thoroughly researched defenses of the book's historical claims. Nevertheless, if the scholarly conversation is to continue, it has to begin addressing other questions about the Book of Mormon. There's so much to be understood about the Book of Mormon that has so far gone untouched. However, now these other questions are not only of *real* spiritual import, they're of *increasing* spiritual import. What drives many Book of Mormon scholars today, it seems, is a worry that an exclusive concern for just the one question of historicity might compromise the much larger apologetic task. They want a book that's true and valuable not only because it's historical (although that's obviously important). They want a book that's true in a hundred other ways also, and in ways that matter to human beings on an existential and not just on an intellectual level. Their experience leads them to believe that questions beyond that of historicity are what many or even most readers of the Book of Mormon want answers to. As we've said before, readers of the Book of Mormon today are as likely—if not in fact *more* likely—to reject the Book of Mormon for reasons that have nothing to do with historicity. They're as likely or more likely to drop the book and the religion endorsing it because the volume seems to them to be irrelevant, archaic, boring, unenlightening, or ethically troubling. This is something we see among our students too often, and there's reason to help a new generation see the book's power that we see.

A simple simile might be useful in expressing what's happening among newer Book of Mormon scholars. Returning again and again to the issue of Book of Mormon historicity can feel like starting a car in the garage over and over again to prove that it runs—but only seldom putting the thing into drive to see what it might do. Book of Mormon researchers today increasingly feel that it's time to trust all the evidence that the car runs and take it out onto the road. How does it handle when the rubber meets the road? Where might a tank of gas in this marvelous vehicle take us? Eagerness to get out of the garage and onto the street doesn't begin from any desire to deny that the car runs. This eagerness is to take as fact that the car runs and then give others outside the garage an opportunity to see what the thing can do. Others deciding that they'd like to take a ride in the car with us isn't a sign that we've somehow compromised the vehicle's integrity. It's a sign, we hope, that the car has more to recommend it than we've ever realized.

There's reason, then, to celebrate new developments in Book of Mormon scholarship, even as there's reason to celebrate the incredible

> "At some point, I realized that I had been avoiding the Book of Mormon for years because I was afraid that it would not be complex and rewarding. I was afraid that it would not measure up—that I would find it simplistic and immature—and I was not sure that my adult faith could withstand that discovery."
>
> —Michael Austin, *Buried Treasures: Reading the Book of Mormon Again for the First Time*

work that's been done by those whose shoulders Book of Mormon scholars stand on today. We fully appreciate those who worked professionally over the course of six or seven decades to set the Book of Mormon in the ancient world and who proved themselves to be astonishingly prolific and creative in their efforts. They scoured the records of the human race, sifted through the sands of ancient civilizations, mastered dozens of languages, and discerned new ways of reading the text. The monument to the Book of Mormon they built is a wonder, breathtaking in its scope. And now, we believe, there's good and faithful reason to muster exactly the same kind of commitment and ingenuity and put that into a host of other questions regarding the book's truth. If we had a small army of trained theologians, reception historians, textual critics, literary scholars, and social critics all working as hard on the Book of Mormon as those trained in ancient history have worked before us, what might emerge from their effort and inventiveness? And the good news is that precisely such a small army has perhaps begun to take shape and is hard at work in laying the foundations for an expanded field of Book of Mormon studies.

With all that prologue, then, what might be said by way of closing about the newest issues emerging in Book of Mormon scholarship? What's begun to take shape that invites the careful attention of the next generation? And how does this mark a change, all over again, from what's happened in the past even as it continues in the broader apologetic spirit that's animated Book of Mormon studies from the beginning?

QUESTIONS OF IDENTITY

It isn't surprising that, in the political climate of the past decade in the United States of America, the question of race in the Book of Mormon has received increasing emphasis. This isn't simply due to a changing political culture, however, as if it were merely a secular concern. Leaders of the Church have emphasized more and more strongly the importance of working for the elimination of racism from the world and from Latter-day Saint culture. It's thus partially in direct response to a prophetic call that at least some scholars working on race in the Book of Mormon take up their task. Because some within the Church have occasionally used scripture—including the Book of Mormon—to justify racist attitudes or defend racist structures, there's a strong need for a more careful assessment of what the Book of Mormon has to say about racism and racialism. Numerous passages seem to refer straightforwardly to black or dark skin or to white skin, tying these to differently valued cultures (whiteness to industry, for example, and blackness to idleness). Such passages speak of black skin as a curse, as loathsome and unattractive, and as something to be overcome. In addition, there's a long history of racist verbal and pictorial portrayals of the Book of Mormon's Lamanites that has often cemented attitudes about what's at stake racially in the volume, not to mention the very real and painful toll such depictions have taken on people of color within and outside the Church.

Of course, these difficulties haven't come into visibility only in the twenty-first century. Readers with concerns about potentially troubling passages about race in the Book of Mormon have offered creative interpretations since the 1950s and 1960s at least. The most common approach to dealing creatively with such passages during the last decades of the twentieth century was to argue that talk of blackness and whiteness in the volume is wholly or ultimately metaphorical. According to this approach, the book probably doesn't deal with questions of race at all but rather with two racially identical peoples who use color-based metaphors to speak of righteousness and wickedness. While this is

New Directions

> "I grieve that our Black brothers and sisters the world over are enduring the pains of racism and prejudice. Today I call upon our members everywhere to lead out in abandoning attitudes and actions of prejudice."
>
> —Russell M. Nelson, "Let God Prevail," October 2020 general conference

a possible and interesting explanation of the text (and has received provocative new support in certain recent quarters), few seem content with this approach today. There are passages in the Book of Mormon that are simply too hard to explain as merely metaphorical. And even if one might work up creative ways of explaining as metaphorical every potentially difficult passage, the fact is that most readers don't generally receive them that way. Latter-day Saints sitting in the pews continue to be most often led by the surface meaning of the text to assume that the book makes claims about races and skin color. Further, some point out that, even if all the potentially troubling passages were merely metaphorical, it has to be recognized that even metaphors have cultural implications and a social impact that can't be ignored. Numerous passages in the Book of Mormon set up whiteness and white skin, even if only symbolically, as a kind of ideal standard, and this says something to readers who experience their skin color as an object of scorn or shame.

The consensus that's begun to emerge among scholars in recent years is that the Book of Mormon almost certainly talks—and talks in straightforward ways—about race and racialism. There are key passages in the book, in fact, where certain prophetic voices explicitly identify racism (hatred because of skin color, as well as the attribution of cultural associations to race), calling it a sin and condemning the Nephites for exhibiting it. It thus seems that the Book of Mormon *shows* racism to its readers, even as it simultaneously *condemns* it. It presents the history of a people that were often racist, the Nephites, and it asks its readers to watch as prophets struggle from within racist cultures to allow God's own anti-racism to reveal itself. In addition, the Book of Mormon places at a key point in the narrative a prophet of color, Samuel the Lamanite, the only Book of Mormon prophet quoted by the resurrected Christ during his visit to the New World. Where Nephite prophets struggle from within a racist culture—sometimes themselves using racializing language—this Lamanite prophet issues a clear call for systemic change and individual repentance. With these interpretive frameworks in place, the beginnings of a sustained faithful engagement with race and the Book of Mormon are seriously underway.

Another issue that has been increasingly emphasized in recent years in Book of Mormon studies is gender. After the rise of feminism as a mainstream cultural and political force, it has become difficult for readers of the Book of Mormon not to notice how few female characters there are in the volume—and how often women in the book face physical and sexual violence. Only three uniquely Book of Mormon women have names, and few of the Book of Mormon's women receive any opportunity to have their voices heard by others. Although readers can celebrate Sariah, the matriarch of the Book of Mormon's opening book, 1 Nephi, and Abish, the Lamanite heroine who plays a key role during the conversion of the Anti-Nephi-Lehies, most of the Book of Mormon seems at least superficially uninterested in women, unless it's occasionally to recount their sufferings. In the context of increasing gender equity in Latter-day Saint culture during the twenty-first century, these textual matters have grown in cultural importance.

Study of gender in the Book of Mormon also has twentieth-century precedents. In the wake of American feminism in the 1960s and 1970s, studies of women in the Book of Mormon occasionally appeared during the 1980s and 1990s—some more obviously liberal and some more obviously conservative. Most of these twentieth-century publications, although they were largely written by believing readers, brought a harshly critical eye to the text, surveying the violent fates of women in the narrative and lamenting the androcentric nature of most of the text. Most historicized these issues, taking the poor representation of women in the book to be a feature of the volume's antiquity, its origins long before the

> **WOMEN WHO ARE NAMED IN THE BOOK OF MORMON**
>
> · Sariah
> · Eve
> · Abish
> · Sarah
> · Isabel
> · Mary

rise of Western feminism. A few called for a strong historicization, an explicit rejection of the spiritual relevance—at least in terms of gender—of a text hailing from a misogynistic era. Others called for a kind of compassion toward the authors and editors of the book, whether because they didn't know better or because they overlooked women as they gave their attention to other spiritual purposes.

Recent years have seen not only an uptick in the frequency and length of publications on women in the Book of Mormon but also a broadening of the subject of gender in the Book of Mormon and the emergence of new approaches to interpreting passages in the book regarding gender. The last few years have thus seen the first studies of masculinity in the Book of Mormon, along with studies of how the volume portrays and understands the very category of women. They have also seen the first intersectional studies—that is, studies of how race and gender are interrelated in the Book of Mormon. Further, though, in connection with intersectional research, there has emerged an approach to gender in the Book of Mormon that's not unlike the recent approach to race in the volume. Interpreters point to the possibility that the book is meant to illustrate a misogynistic Nephite culture and to show that such a culture leads ultimately to social and cultural ruin: the destruction of the Nephites. These interpreters note that women consistently fare better in Lamanite culture and that the Lamanites remain alive at the end of the volume, surviving to receive further blessings. There's real and compelling evidence that the Book of Mormon has been deliberately shaped to show how a racist and misogynistic people destroy themselves while those who resist both racism and misogyny find divine help and preservation. Here again, Samuel the Lamanite is a particularly interesting figure. Not only is he a prophet of color, but he also speaks forcefully in behalf of Nephite women in Helaman 15, recognizing parallels between their plights and those of his own racialized people. Here again, with the basic foundation for gendered study of the Book of Mormon in place, close and charitable readings of the Book of Mormon's presentation of women and men have begun to appear.

As we mentioned in chapter 2, yet another issue has only just begun to receive real interest in Book of Mormon studies: the question of what the volume might say about mental health issues and about disabilities.

Increased attention to this is unmistakably due to growing social recognition of these issues in the twenty-first century. The very first clearly recognizable disability studies reading of the Book of Mormon appeared two decades into the twenty-first century, but it promises to be the first of many. In a more general vein, though, late 1990s readings of the theme of grace in the Book of Mormon helped draw the attention of twenty-first-century readers to the volume's consistent interest in weakness. Key figures in the Book of Mormon—Nephi, Jacob, Benjamin, Alma, and Moroni—overtly confess and confront their weakness and even develop theological reflections on the way that weakness might be a gift. That human frailty in this way extends even to mental and psychological trauma is clear from passages about the mourning of whole communities in the wake of terrible battles; it's also clear in a particularly rich way in what may be Moroni's symptoms of post-traumatic stress disorder when he first takes up the task of writing in the book after the final Nephite wars and his father's death. The Book of Mormon offers itself up to those with concerns about mental health, and it has just begun to receive real attention from such readers in Book of Mormon studies—once again with the promise of more to come.

QUESTIONS OF POLITICS

A number of other issues of increasing importance to twenty-first-century readers have begun to draw attention in Book of Mormon studies, as we summarized briefly in chapter 2. Already in the twentieth century, the Book of Mormon's many descriptions of war and violence prompted concern from some readers. Several writers attempted to explain how the book might be read as endorsing a peacebuilding ethic, if not a pacifist stance regarding war and violence. FARMS scholars in the 1990s took, for the most part, a different tack, leaving off questions of whether the book's portrayal of sustained warfare is relevant to the modern audience and investigating instead whether its descriptions of war fit well into what's known of ancient warfare. Questions about what the Book of Mormon says of war have, however, begun to garner more widespread interest in the twenty-first century. Thanks in part to the politically divisive spirit in the United States of America during the first decades of the twenty-first century, students of the Book of Mormon

New Directions

> "Nephi's struggle, and the struggle of his descendants, is one to which any reader can relate. Faced with conflict, do we turn to loving persuasion or angry coercion to resolve our differences? Like Nephi it can be easy to despair of our personal or cultural affinities for anger and violence, to be discouraged with our 'wretched' patterns of conflict. But the Book of Mormon testifies that there is another, better way available to us."
>
> —Patrick Q. Mason and John David Pulsipher, *Proclaim Peace: The Restoration's Answer to an Age of Conflict*

---

addressing questions about warfare in the book have tended to take polar opposite positions. Some scholars express deep concern about the book's proclivity for violence, and others argue intently that the book rightly endorses war as necessary and righteous under certain circumstances. (Concerns about violence in war often extend to particular stories about violence, such as Laban's death early in 1 Nephi.)

Related in many ways to questions about war and violence in the Book of Mormon are questions about whether and how this sacred scripture should be used in defense of political programs. Growing interest in liberal and progressive readings of the Book of Mormon has led to overt critiques of the figure of Captain Moroni as brash and irascible. Of course, such critiques are consistently countered by readings of Moroni not only as the greatest patriot the Book of Mormon portrays but also as an admirably realistic strategist with clear Christian commitments. Several new readers of the Book of Mormon in recent years have begun to ask earnestly what the concrete sociopolitical situations on display in the Book of Mormon look like and what the book's message regarding latter-day politics might be. More nuanced readings of the strictly political dimension of the book are largely in their infancy, with the vast majority of what's said or written on the subject too ideologically divided by prior political commitments. But the field of Book of Mormon studies as a scholarly discipline has begun to foster political readings undertaken with great care and with a moderate spirit. What might the Book of Mormon's comments about the voice of the people really suggest about the power of political rhetoric? How might Mormon's intense interest in just a few years of the reign of the judges clarify his own political purposes? What does a nuanced reading of King Benjamin's concern for his people or his son's criticisms of monarchy have to say about political institutions?

King Benjamin's sermon is often a focus in reflections on problems of poverty and in reflections more generally on questions of class. To date, no sustained or careful study of the question of poverty in the Book of Mormon has appeared, although there's clear interest in it. It's perfectly clear to any reader of the Book of Mormon that the prophets who populate its pages have concerns about wealth—at the very least about wealth wrongly acquired or wrongly disposed. It's also perfectly clear to any reader of the Book of Mormon that the Nephite prophets believed strongly that prosperity comes, at least at times, in response to human righteousness. Book of Mormon peoples live best when they hold all things in common, and their utopian civilization after Christ's visit falls apart when classes reemerge as central to their society. And yet the Book of Mormon prescribes no obvious or consistent program for how to eliminate problems of poverty. Increasing interest in these questions, intensified in key ways by the Church's explicit expression of interest in refugees and victims of natural disasters, suggests that textual work on such questions needs to begin in earnest. That there are the merest beginnings of this kind of work in Book of Mormon studies is a sign that a significant wing of the field is beginning to take shape.

QUESTIONS OF MEANING

The several issues reviewed in the previous two sections constitute points where the text of the Book of Mormon is already being critiqued or is more likely to be critiqued in the near future. They're points where specific challenges to the Book of Mormon have begun to receive new and refreshing answers. The reality is that readers suffering from severe depression are less likely to be worried about whether the Book of Mormon meets the historical standards set by contemporary consensus

> "In terms of word count, slightly more than sixty percent of the words in [King Benjamin's] discussion of the fruits of repentance are about how we respond to the beggar and others in need. Clearly this is an important topic for Benjamin."
>
> —James E. Faulconer, *Mosiah: A Brief Theological Introduction*

scholarship than about whether it can speak to them peaceably, without burdening them more than they're already burdened psychologically. A reader with intense worries about political instability and growing political polarization is less likely to balk at the lack of a recognizable geographic model that fits the Book of Mormon than at the book's apparent readiness to be politically appropriated by extremist groups. Readers of color, as well as white readers increasingly concerned with combating racism in the twenty-first century, are far more likely to fret over the Book of Mormon's discussions of skin color than about traces of the King James Bible in the volume. And readers with growing awareness of gender and sexual inequities are strikingly more concerned with the apparent absence of women in the Book of Mormon than they are with whether it's possible to find Hebraic poetic patterns scattered about the text. The Book of Mormon is implicitly under fire, so to speak, from a host of new angles. The new vision gaining ground in Book of Mormon studies is working to address these issues, to show not only that the Book of Mormon can hold its ground on all these twenty-first-century questions but also that the book might have much to teach us as we try to negotiate the difficult terrain we all now find ourselves on.

In addition to specific critiques of the Book of Mormon in the twenty-first century, though, there's a kind of general and implicit critique. And right at present, this critique might form the most immediate concern in budding twenty-first-century Book of Mormon studies. The question here is whether the book is, to put it bluntly, *boring*. Long before readers raise questions about gender and race, about politics and mental health, about violence and poverty, they tend to raise questions about whether the Book of Mormon is worth reading *at all*. In the twenty-first century, with secularism becoming culturally normative and religion becoming an increasingly private affair, many have begun simply to ask whether religion in any form (and especially organized forms) is worth the bother. And when religion involves reading over and over an unsubtle and didactic book filled with "thees" and "thous" and "it came to passes"—especially if it doesn't seem that the book has anything unsurprising to say about the life of faith—one rather naturally begins to ask in a secular context whether the book really *matters* in the twenty-first century. What's perhaps most characteristic of twenty-first-century Book of Mormon studies, then, is a widespread effort to show that the Book of Mormon is rich and provocative, that it's filled with literary and theological surprises. Much of the effort expended in recent scholarship, as we've summarized less directly in early chapters, is aimed at showing that the Book of Mormon is filled with things as yet undiscovered, and that serious investigation of the book has only just begun.

That the Book of Mormon is simply boring, irrelevant, clichéd, or uninformative threatens to be the most uncontested of slam dunks against the book today (to use Elder Maxwell's metaphor again).[1] The player on the court who's trying to show off with this slam dunk, though, isn't an individual. It's rather a whole twenty-first-century secular culture, the entirety of an increasingly irreligious world. This is a slam dunk that can't be ignored a moment longer, and it's in hoping to contest it that the best work in Book of Mormon studies today is being pursued. How might we show that the Book of Mormon is not only relevantly defensible in political and ethical terms in the twenty-first-century context but also of deep and sustained interest to anyone who will take it seriously? In the twentieth century, it seems it was possible to defend the Book of Mormon principally by showing that its historicity is defensible. If there weren't compelling historical reasons to disbelieve the book's claims, it was worth holding on to one's faith. In the twenty-first century, though, historicity is only one among many key concerns. We must show that the book has real force.

The greatest *active* successes in Book of Mormon studies today (rather than its principally *reactive* successes) therefore have been neither in discerning new defenses of the book's antiquity nor in responding to increasingly felt cultural criticisms of the book's content. What's

> "Mark Twain, who once memorably referred to the Book of Mormon as 'chloroform in print,' is also our source for the quip that Wagner's music is 'better than it sounds.' Somewhat surprisingly, it may actually be the latter description that more accurately describes the Book of Mormon. There is no denying that the words can sound awkward, repetitious, and derivative, but if we direct our attention deeper, to the level of form and structure, there is much more going on than first meets the eye (or ear)."
>
> —Grant Hardy, *Understanding the Book of Mormon: A Reader's Guide*

pressing the book's way into the future is work that's successfully showing that the Book of Mormon is rich and complex, that it has unexpected theological commitments, that it has intricate structures that organize its ideas and teachings, that it traces certain ideas across generations while suggesting that other ideas come and go, that it can speak to the most burning theological questions of the Christian tradition, that it can stand robustly alongside the greatest volumes of world scripture, and that it can bear the most scrutinizing literary investigation.

Scholars have begun to show that the Book of Mormon's various authors have distinct projects and visions—that Nephi and Mormon and Moroni are wholly different kinds of writers, each with his own hopes and anxieties. Scholars have begun to show that the Book of Mormon emphasizes the theme of Israel's covenant in a way that's surprising to most Latter-day Saints, with remarkably novel interpretations of Old Testament scripture. Scholars have begun to show how the Book of Mormon reworks major New Testament themes in virtuosic ways, sketching a unique scriptural theology that's gone unnoticed for most of the Church's history. Scholars have begun to show that the Book of Mormon endorses a nuanced and rich Christology and a theology of grace that has deeply important practical implications for the life of faith. The Book of Mormon is increasingly revealing its relevance and force.

Above and right: *The Book of Mormon: Brief Theological Introductions*

Courtesy of the Neal A. Maxwell Institute for Religious Scholarship

The future of Book of Mormon studies finds its point of orientation in all this sort of work. What's taking shape is an abundance of work showing how the Book of Mormon—alongside direction from living prophets, of course—might help guide the Saints through the shifting sands of twenty-first-century political culture. And along with this, an ever-deeper sense of what the Book of Mormon's own theological commitments are—the picture the book tries to paint for its latter-day readers—is growing. For most or all of the twentieth century, it was thought that the Book of Mormon's Achilles' heel was the question of historicity, and so believing scholars worked hard to keep arrows from penetrating that one vulnerable place. Today, however, it's become clear that many other parts of the Book of Mormon are exposed to danger, and believing scholars are working hard to provide the book with armor—and to show that the Book of Mormon's own skin might be armor enough, if the book is read carefully. And questions of whether the book can continue to be meaningful in the life of the Saints, of whether the book might in fact prove more meaningful than any of us

DEFINITION

Christology:
Theological reflection on the nature of Christ, particularly the fusion of divinity and humanity in the person of Jesus of Nazareth.

imagined it could be, are the ones being asked with the most intensity. This makes for a genuinely bright future.

NOTE

1. See Gilbert W. Scharffs, "I Have a Question," *Ensign*, January 1995, 62.

Conclusion

In 1869 the first transcontinental railroad in the United States was completed. For two decades, the Saints in and around Utah had been able to largely create their own culture and live as they wished. There had been enemies in their midst, of course, and often enough outsiders came through and raised uncomfortable questions that the Saints had to provide good answers to. But a new era dawned with the completion of the railroad. The buffer between the Saints and the rest of the United States disappeared, and it became necessary to think up new strategies for interacting with people who quickly became neighbors instead of enemies. Members of the Church had to develop new ways of talking about their faith that would allow them to get along with other Americans without compromising their commitments to the faith of their pioneer mothers and fathers.

Something like a transcontinental railroad has been completed in the last two decades—one that connects traditional study of the Book of Mormon to the larger scholarly world and the concerns that often animate it. We might react to this development in any variety of ways, but the reality is that young members of the Church are increasingly

Driving the golden spike at Promontory Summit, Utah Territory, May 10, 1869.

familiar with those concerns at the other end of that railroad—as familiar with all that as they are with the Book of Mormon at this end of the same set of tracks. The way we study the Book of Mormon when we do our most serious intellectual work on it *will* change, and we have to decide what that change will look like. We need not—and in fact must not—give up on the truth of the Book of Mormon—on its spiritual truth or on its historical truth. But how we talk about and defend that truth is already changing. Some questions that seemed pressing just a few years ago seem less pressing today, while questions that didn't seem terribly important just a few years ago seem crucial today.

In this book, we've tried to outline what it means for believing scholars to be regular passengers on the train that goes back and forth between academic and devotional study of the Book of Mormon. We haven't tried to provide a final word on these matters. Far from it! If anything, we've tried to speak just a *first* word, to announce that the situation looks different today, and to ask for understanding as we and others come to explore the contours of the altered terrain. And we hope we've sounded an invitation to other faithful scholars (and budding scholars)

Conclusion

to find their way to the station platform. Come and help us figure out how this dawning project will work—in full fidelity to the Restoration and with total academic rigor, by study and by faith. There are many empty seats on the train, and we'd love the company. For those interested in reading about the journey but uninterested in getting on the train, we hope we've made the case that there's much to be learned from what's happening. Exciting times lie ahead, and there's every reason to be watching for news about discoveries in Book of Mormon studies. And for those interested in (or already) working on the Book of Mormon from outside the bounds of the confessional faith, we frankly hope we haven't made things awkward by explaining our reasons of faith for pursuing our work along with you.

In the meanwhile, it's our witness and testimony that the Book of Mormon is true, historically *and* theologically. It's a book that doesn't need to be handled delicately or kept on the shelf. It needs, rather, to be studied. Study always involves risk, but we're convinced that the risk is worth it and that many are up to the challenge. There's much to be gained, including the confidence of young members of the Church in the Book of Mormon. There's much to be lost as well, so it's crucial that believing scholars try to be cautious, eyes peeled and always aware so that they are thorough, honest, and undogmatic in their work. Mistakes will certainly be made (thank the heavens for grace!). So long as we carry an unshakable conviction of the unswerving truth of the Restoration with us, though, we can trust that God will be with the scholars seeking to understand the foundation of our shared faith.

We're still in the midst of the divine coming forth of the Book of Mormon. Let's pray that this is another important stage of that marvelous work and wonder.

> It's our witness and testimony that the Book of Mormon is true, historically *and* theologically. It's a book that doesn't need to be handled delicately or kept on the shelf. It needs, rather, to be studied.

Appendix

As we explained in the introduction, the purpose of this appendix is to serve as a guide to books, articles, and institutions relevant to students of the Book of Mormon. Citation information for every book and essay we've referred or alluded to in the previous pages can be found here, in most cases alongside a little further information about what's important about the source in question. There's also some helpful information about each of the institutions that promote, publish, or otherwise support Book of Mormon studies. The appendix is divided into five parts: (1) "Getting Started," a quick guide to the essential works coming out of Book of Mormon studies, which is the kind of thing we'd recommend to absolutely anyone hoping to learn more; (2) "Getting Serious," an introduction to the books and essays that anyone serious about contributing to Book of Mormon studies should read or become familiar with, regardless of her or his specialization; (3) "Getting Specialized," an outline of works that can't be missed by anyone getting involved in this or that specialization within Book of Mormon studies; (4) "Getting Around," a quick guide to the institutions that serve and support the

Appendix

field; and (5) "Other Sources We've Cited along the Way," a list of other sources we've mentioned that aren't found elsewhere in the appendix.

What follows here is by no means exhaustive. It is, though, relatively comprehensive. That is, it ought to be enough to get anyone oriented in the field without any major gaps. Of course, specialization always requires going further into the literature, but we hope this appendix lights the first several yards of each road leading to a specific specialization.

PART 1: GETTING STARTED

Everything we've talked about in the preceding chapters might seem a bit overwhelming, and so the very idea of Book of Mormon studies might now feel daunting. To ease the burden, here we'd like to lay out the essential works in Book of Mormon studies—the kinds of things that *anyone*—student, scholar, or lay reader alike—might immediately benefit from. The list is short, and it should be all you need to begin to find your way into the unwieldy world of scholarship we've tried to summarize in this book.

First, there are two editions of the Book of Mormon itself with which even a beginning student of the Book of Mormon ought to be familiar. By far the most important scholarly edition of the book is **Royal Skousen, ed.,** *The Book of Mormon: The Earliest Text* (New Haven: Yale University Press, 2009). This edition is the finished product of literally decades of research on the manuscripts for and every major printed edition of the Book of Mormon. Professor Skousen gave years to the task of tracking down every variant among the manuscripts and editions and then analyzing these variants in depth to decide what their significance might be for establishing a critical text. (The details of all this labor are found in *Analysis of Textual Variants of the Book of Mormon*, discussed in part 2 below, and *The History of the Text of the Book of Mormon*, discussed in part 3 below.) Skousen's *Earliest Text* thus contains what he estimates to be the actual words spoken by Joseph Smith during the dictation of the Book of Mormon to his scribes. In Book of Mormon scholarship, it's now more or less standard to quote from this edition. The edition is easy to read. Scholarly apparatus (such as a list of major differences among editions and manuscripts) is relegated to an appendix, and the text is laid out in "sense lines" that arguably make reading the text more natural. Skousen's work has made clear how much serious academic study of the Book of Mormon must be informed by a reliable edition of the text.

As anyone familiar with the Book of Mormon knows, the translated book has a peculiar origin story—involving angels and plates, miraculous gifts of translation and scholars hoping to open sealed books, and difficulties surrounding finances and manual printing labor. Really, though, every student of the Book of Mormon ought to be far more familiar with all these details of history. By far the best resource for becoming familiar with the translation history of the Book of Mormon is a book written specifically for believing Latter-day Saints: **Michael Hubbard MacKay and Gerrit J. Dirkmaat,** *From Darkness unto Light: Joseph Smith's Translation and Publication of the Book of Mormon* (Provo, UT: Religious Studies Center, Brigham Young University; Salt Lake City, UT: Deseret Book, 2015). MacKay and Dirkmaat, currently professors in the Department of Church History and Doctrine at Brigham Young University (BYU), are both former contributors to the Joseph Smith Papers Project. Their study of the coming forth of the Book of Mormon therefore demonstrates astonishing intimacy with original historical sources, and it brings out many details about these events that are less familiar to the Saints. Without reading this book, one doesn't know the full story of how the Book of Mormon came into the world in the latter days.

After its translation and initial publication, the Book of Mormon almost immediately became the object of intense devotion and furious attack. There has followed a long and complex history of nearly two hundred years, during which the Book of Mormon has not only been loved and hated but also carefully interpreted and editorially repackaged, represented in art and made into film, translated into many languages, and used in a variety of ways in curriculum and missionary labors. A brilliant historical summary of the Book of Mormon's uses and abuses since its first publication is found in **Paul C. Gutjahr,** *The Book of Mormon: A Biography* (Princeton: Princeton University Press, 2012). Gutjahr isn't a member of The Church of Jesus Christ of Latter-day Saints, but he takes great care with the sacred text and tells the story of its "biography" most

Appendix

responsibly. Gutjahr's book is not only a key orienting work of reception history for scholars but also a solid introduction for any student of the Book of Mormon to how the book has fared over the first two centuries of its circulation. This is a must-read for anyone interested in the Book of Mormon in a serious way.

Another key work in reception history—although with different stakes and a narrower focus—is **Terryl L. Givens, *By the Hand of Mormon: The American Scripture That Launched a New World Religion*** (New York: Oxford University Press, 2002). Givens's book has proved deeply important not only for Book of Mormon studies more narrowly but also for the whole larger field going by the name of "Mormon studies." The book tracks the specifically *intellectual* history of the Book of Mormon's reception—the good and the bad, and in substantial detail. Moreover, this book is arguably the one that sealed off twentieth-century Book of Mormon studies through its celebration of the successes of the Foundation for Ancient Research and Mormon Studies (FARMS) and the one that inaugurated twenty-first-century Book of Mormon studies by landing itself with Oxford University Press. Givens doesn't have much to say about the text of the Book of Mormon itself (although some parts of the book do look at passages in detail). What's of interest to him is where the book fits into the Restoration and why it's important that the book has served as the principal evidence for the truth of Joseph Smith's role as prophet. No one serious about Book of Mormon studies in the twenty-first century can avoid grappling with Givens's presentation of the Book of Mormon's place and stakes.

Finally, there's one book on the actual content of the Book of Mormon that unquestionably ought to be read by everyone seriously interested in scholarly study of the Book of Mormon. This is **Grant Hardy, *Understanding the Book of Mormon: A Reader's Guide*** (New York: Oxford University Press, 2010). Building on the close reading that went into creating his earlier ***Reader's Edition*** (dealt with in detail in part 2 below), Hardy's *Understanding the Book of Mormon* is without question the most important single book published to date on the Book of Mormon. It has been astonishingly influential for twenty-first-century Book of Mormon studies. In terms of method, Hardy approaches the text with a narratological perspective, asking how the

Book of Mormon's authors and editors go about telling their stories. The result is a careful analysis of the volume's three major contributors: Nephi, Mormon, and Moroni—each with his own interests and style, purpose and hopes. Hardy carefully lays aside worries about defending or attacking the historicity of the Book of Mormon and instead asks just what the book says and how it says it. Hardy's book not only has raised Latter-day Saint scholarship on the Book of Mormon to a new level but also has been a key invitation to non–Latter-day Saint scholars to read the book in earnest. Every student of the Book of Mormon must be familiar with *Understanding the Book of Mormon*.

PART 2: GETTING SERIOUS

If you're quite familiar already with the materials discussed in part 1, you might feel that you're ready to get serious about Book of Mormon studies. What in the field—at least as it's currently constituted—should *every* earnest student of the Book of Mormon be familiar with? What comes next? There's of course so much more written on the Book of Mormon than anyone can get to in a reasonable amount of time, so what's worth privileging? To answer these questions and so to construct part 2 of this appendix, we've asked ourselves a simple question: What works in Book of Mormon studies would anyone presenting a scholarly paper at a conference or submitting a scholarly paper for publication on the book be *expected* to be familiar with? Of course, depending on what one speaks or writes about, there might be specialized publications of particular relevance one would need to know. But the question here is what *everyone* writing on the Book of Mormon is expected to know. That's a hard question to answer. We've had to make some judgment calls in answering it. What follows, though, is nonetheless a helpful place to get moving.

We recommended one particular edition of the Book of Mormon in part 1, which is a standard source for those working in the field and is simultaneously accessible to nonscholars. Here we might recommend two other editions. The first is **Grant Hardy, ed.,** ***The Book of Mormon: Another Testament of Jesus Christ, Maxwell Institute Study Edition*** (Provo, UT: Neal A. Maxwell Institute for Religious Scholarship; Religious Studies Center, Brigham Young University; Salt Lake City, UT:

Deseret Book, 2018). The second is something like an earlier version of this: **Grant Hardy, ed.,** *The Book of Mormon: A Reader's Edition* (Urbana: University of Illinois Press, 2003). This earlier effort was deliberately aimed at assisting non–Latter-day Saint readers and introducing the Book of Mormon to the larger scholarly world. After some years, however, Hardy returned to the task of producing a useful edition of the Book of Mormon, this time with the deliberate aim to make the book more accessible and useful to Latter-day Saint readers, scholarly and nonscholarly alike. The *Maxwell Institute Study Edition* uses the current official text of the Book of Mormon but resets the text in readable paragraphs and (where it's amenable) poetic stanzas. Footnotes explain major textual variants, key details within the text's structure, direct citations or borrowings from other passages, and basic issues of chronology. A series of deeply useful appendices concludes the volume, with maps and genealogies, statements by witnesses to the translation, and some general introductions to a few key issues in Book of Mormon studies. The book is beautiful to boot, including gorgeous artwork by Brian Kershisnik created for the volume.

While we're talking about editions, a key resource for understanding the publishing history of the text of the Book of Mormon—a guide to historical editions—is **Richard E. Turley Jr. and William W. Slaughter,** *How We Got the Book of Mormon* (Salt Lake City: Deseret Book, 2011). Turley and Slaughter write for a general audience rather than a scholarly one, and they assume a readership made up of believing Latter-day Saints. They provide a wonderfully helpful orientation.

A few standard reference materials are crucial. The most comprehensive commentary yet published on the Book of Mormon is **Brant A. Gardner,** *Second Witness: Analytical and Contextual Commentary on the Book of Mormon*, 6 vols. (Salt Lake City: Greg Kofford Books, 2007). Gardner leans heavily in a historical direction, and especially a Mesoamerican direction, but his wide-ranging commentary takes in a variety of approaches. He also usefully sifts twentieth-century scholarship as he comments on the text, more or less verse by verse. Another helpful resource for sifting twentieth-century sources is the encyclopedia-like **Dennis L. Largey, ed.,** *Book of Mormon Reference Companion* (Salt Lake City: Deseret Book, 2003). Entries in the *Reference Companion* are authored by a variety of different scholars, the vast majority of them from BYU's Religious Education faculty. Gardner's and Largey's works are thus good places to check to see what's been said on just about any topic or passage in the Book of Mormon before proceeding to one's own work. Also useful for sifting twentieth-century work, by the way—and this time with a specific focus on FARMS's contribution—is **Donald W. Parry, Daniel C. Peterson, and John W. Welch, eds.,** *Echoes and Evidences of the Book of Mormon* (Provo, UT: FARMS, 2002). This book is a collection of essays, each of which is written by a major FARMS scholar and summarizes FARMS research on some specific dimension of the Book of Mormon.

A particularly important reference work is **Royal Skousen,** *Analysis of Textual Variants of the Book of Mormon*, 6 vols., 2nd ed. (Provo, UT: BYU Studies; FARMS, 2017). This set of six large volumes contains Skousen's notes on more or less every variant in the Book of Mormon's print history. They're essentially the notes produced along the way as Skousen worked to publish *The Book of Mormon: The Earliest Text*, mentioned already in part 1. Because Skousen occasionally makes judgment calls in constructing *The Earliest Text*, it's crucial for serious students of the Book of Mormon to be familiar with the details lying behind his now-standard edition. (Remember that some of the more significant variants are highlighted in *The Earliest Text* itself in an appendix, as well as in the footnotes of Hardy's *Maxwell Institute Study Edition* of the Book of Mormon.) One further reference work of sorts that certainly deserves notice here is **Terryl L. Givens,** *The Book of Mormon: A Very Short Introduction* (New York: Oxford University Press, 2009). Going much deeper into the text of the Book of Mormon than *By the Hand of Mormon*, this little volume gives an overview of the text from a theological angle. It's a likely place for many non–Latter-day Saints to start, and so it's crucial for serious students of the Book of Mormon to know it well.

Since 2018, in each issue the *Journal of Book of Mormon Studies* has published a detailed review of literature on some specialized topic within Book of Mormon studies. These reviews have quickly become key resources for all students of the Book of Mormon and a starting place for further research. They are key reference works in their own right and include—so far—**Russell W. Stevenson, "Reckoning with Race in the Book of Mormon: A Review of Literature,"** *Journal of Book of Mormon Studies* 27 (2018): 210–25; **Nicholas J. Frederick, "The Bible and the Book of Mormon: A Review of Literature,"** *Journal of Book of Mormon Studies* 28 (2019): 205–36; **Joseph M. Spencer, "The Presentation of Gender in the Book of Mormon: A Review of Literature,"** *Journal of Book of Mormon Studies* 29 (2020): 231–63; and **Scott Hales, "Something Akin to Dissatisfaction: A Review of Book of Mormon Novels,"** *Journal of Book of Mormon Studies* 30 (2021): 198–230. Each issue of the *Journal of Book of Mormon Studies* has also included—since 2017—an annual bibliography of scholarly works on the Book of Mormon published during the previous year. Every scholar working on the Book of Mormon should be perusing these annual bibliographies alongside the literature reviews. Note also that there's a comprehensive bibliography for work published up until the mid-1990s: **Donald W. Parry, Jeanette W. Miller, and Sandra A. Thorne, eds., *A Comprehensive Annotated Book of Mormon Bibliography*** (Provo, UT: FARMS, 1996).

A few works on the early history of the Book of Mormon's reception—on how the book was read and understood by the first Latter-day Saints and sometimes by later generations—have profoundly influenced the way that scholars have understood the book's modern history. Of chief importance here (in addition to Givens's *By the Hand of Mormon*, already addressed in part 1) are three treatments: the first chapter of **Philip L. Barlow, *Mormons and the Bible: The Place of the Latter-day Saints in American Religion*** (New York: Oxford University Press, 1991); **Grant Underwood, "Book of Mormon Usage in Early LDS Theology,"** *Dialogue: A Journal of Mormon Thought* 17, no. 3 (Autumn 1984): 35–74; and **Noel B. Reynolds, "The Coming Forth of the Book of Mormon in the Twentieth Century,"** *BYU Studies Quarterly* 38, no. 2 (1999): 6–47. Recent work that has garnered much attention and begun to qualify and clarify the picture of the Book of Mormon's early reception includes **Janiece Johnson, "Becoming a People of the Books: Toward an Understanding of Early Mormon Converts and the New Word of the Lord,"** *Journal of Book of Mormon Studies* 27 (2018): 1–43.

Appendix

What we've mentioned so far in part 2 are the general works that anyone working in the field of Book of Mormon studies is expected to know. There are also, of course, many works of a more specialized nature that have been influential enough to shape a lot of what's being written on the Book of Mormon in all areas. These therefore deserve the attention of all serious students of the Book of Mormon, whatever specialized topics they work on. We might begin with a few works that are substantially older than others. To start, then, all students of the Book of Mormon ought to be familiar with the writings and approaches of Hugh W. Nibley and Sidney B. Sperry. Although several of their works can be found in parts 3 and 5 of this appendix, some particularly important ones that can quickly familiarize students with their work are **Hugh Nibley, *Since Cumorah*,** 2nd ed., vol. 7 of *The Collected Works of Hugh Nibley* (Provo, UT: FARMS; Salt Lake City, UT: Deseret Book, 1988); and **Sidney B. Sperry, *Our Book of Mormon*** (Salt Lake City: Bookcraft, 1947).

Also important by way of providing context for earlier Book of Mormon studies is **Fawn M. Brodie, *No Man Knows My History: The Life of Joseph Smith*,** 2nd ed. (New York: Vintage Books, 1995). This is, of course, the book that spurred scholars like Nibley and Sperry to write in defense of the Book of Mormon in the first place. References to Brodie's skeptical readings still frequently appear in the literature. A substantial and decidedly more faith-affirming replacement for Brodie's book now exists in the form of **Richard Lyman Bushman, *Joseph Smith: Rough Stone Rolling; A Cultural Biography of Mormonism's Founder*** (New York: Alfred A. Knopf, 2005). This is required reading for anyone working in the larger field of Mormon studies today. An oft-noted attempt to update Brodie's skeptical reading of Joseph Smith's relationship to the Book of Mormon—one that's more invested in addressing the Book of Mormon specifically, in fact—is **Dan Vogel, *Joseph Smith: The Making of a Prophet*** (Salt Lake City: Signature Books, 2004). Also still of serious importance is **D. Michael Quinn, *Early Mormonism and the Magic World View*** (Salt Lake City: Signature Books, 1987), which focuses on the role that folk magic may have played in the circumstances surrounding the coming forth of the Book of Mormon.

Appendix

Two absolutely essential essays—still relevant a half century later—appeared between the time that Nibley and Sperry fell silent on the Book of Mormon and the time when the FARMS era began in earnest. They are too often neglected, but earnest scholars of the Book of Mormon pay them much heed. They are **James H. Charlesworth, "Messianism in the Pseudepigrapha and the Book of Mormon,"** in *Reflections on Mormonism: Judaeo-Christian Parallels*, ed. Truman G. Madsen (Provo, UT: Religious Studies Center, Brigham Young University, 1978), 99–137; and **Krister Stendahl, "The Sermon on the Mount and Third Nephi,"** in *Reflections on Mormonism: Judaeo-Christian Parallels*, ed. Truman G. Madsen (Provo, UT: Religious Studies Center, Brigham Young University, 1978), 139–54. These two works by towering non–Latter-day Saint biblical scholars modeled long in advance the spirit of twenty-first-century Book of Mormon studies, and they both continue to be real spurs to current productive work.

Naturally, there are several works from the FARMS era of Book of Mormon scholarship that have been especially important and should be familiar to all working on the Book of Mormon. Unquestionably, the best-known product of the FARMS scholars is John Welch's work on chiasmus in the Book of Mormon. Welch produced a variety of essays on the subject, and other FARMS scholars (and lay authors) followed up on his discovery with further work of their own. The best introduction to Welch's discovery remains, however, **John W. Welch, "Chiasmus in the Book of Mormon,"** in *Chiasmus in Antiquity: Structures, Analyses, Exegesis*, ed. John W. Welch (Provo, UT: FARMS, 1998), 198–210. (Note that the whole collection in which the essay appears clarifies the status of chiasmus in various ancient contexts.) Of course, FARMS produced many volumes of important work, but the best representative of their collective work—a solid place to become familiar with their general conclusions rather than with the details of their operation—is **John W. Welch and Stephen D. Ricks,** *King Benjamin's Speech: "That Ye May Learn Wisdom"* (Provo, UT: FARMS, 1998). Further, without question, the best twentieth-century work on Mesoamerican connections within the Book of Mormon—also a product of the FARMS project—is **John L. Sorenson,** *An Ancient American Setting for the Book of Mormon* (Provo, UT: FARMS; Salt Lake City, UT: Deseret Book; 1985).

Appendix

As we've noted, the doctrinal project represented by BYU's College of Religious Education was concurrent with FARMS. A particularly representative volume for that whole project would be **Monte S. Nyman and Charles D. Tate Jr., eds.,** *The Book of Mormon: Second Nephi, the Doctrinal Structure* (Provo, UT: Religious Studies Center, Brigham Young University, 1989).

Moving toward the twenty-first century, we've mentioned that questions of translation have been of perennial interest in the history of Book of Mormon studies. These have been admirably summarized in **Grant Hardy, "The Book of Mormon Translation Process,"** *BYU Studies Quarterly* 60, no. 3 (2021): 203–11. Key writings by representatives of the two major theories became essential reading by the early twenty-first century. On the "loose control" end of the spectrum, the still-standard work is **Blake T. Ostler, "The Book of Mormon as a Modern Expansion of an Ancient Source,"** *Dialogue: A Journal of Mormon Thought* 20, no. 1 (Spring 1987): 66–123. On the "tight control" end of the spectrum, the best study remains **Royal Skousen, "Translating the Book of Mormon: Evidence from the Original Manuscript,"** in *Book of Mormon Authorship Revisited: The Evidence for Ancient Origins*, ed. Noel B. Reynolds (Provo, UT: FARMS, 1997), 61–93. Key essays calling for a potential revision of the very idea of translation have appeared quite recently in **Michael Hubbard MacKay, Mark Ashurst-McGee, and Brian M. Hauglid, eds.,** *Producing Ancient Scripture: Joseph Smith's Translation Projects in the Development of Mormon Christianity* (Salt Lake City: University of Utah Press, 2020). For a helpful introduction to the basic mechanics of translation and the key sources, see **Michael Hubbard MacKay and Nicholas J. Frederick,** *Joseph Smith's Seer Stones* (Provo, UT: Religious Studies Center, Brigham Young University; Salt Lake City, UT: Deseret Book, 2016).

Several books stand at the cutting edge of their respective specializations and have drawn much attention. As we've said, each deserves familiarity from anyone working in the field, at the very least in order to have a sense of what's taking shape. On the study of the coming forth of the Book of Mormon, particularly unique and celebrated is **Don Bradley,** *The Lost 116 Pages: Reconstructing the Book of Mormon's Missing Stories* (Salt Lake City: Greg Kofford Books, 2020). Representing the theological angle is **Joseph M. Spencer,** *An Other Testament: On Typology*, 2nd ed. (Provo, UT: Neal A. Maxwell Institute for Religious Scholarship, 2016)—as well as, naturally, the whole ***Book of Mormon: Brief Theological Introductions*** series, edited by J. Spencer Fluhman and Philip L. Barlow and published in 2020 by the Neal A. Maxwell Institute. At the cutting edge of intertextuality stands **Nicholas J. Frederick,** *The Bible, Mormon Scripture, and the Rhetoric of Allusivity* (Madison, NJ: Fairleigh Dickinson University Press, 2016). Pressing the way forward in comparative scripture is unquestionably **Jad Hatem,** *Postponing Heaven: The Three Nephites, the Bodhisattva, and the Mahdi,* **trans. Jonathon Penny** (Provo, UT: Neal A. Maxwell Institute for Religious Scholarship, 2015). Securing the possibilities of a conversation about the Book of Mormon across the borders of different religious traditions is **John Christopher Thomas,** *A Pentecostal Reads the Book of Mormon: A Literary and Theological Introduction* (Cleveland, TN: CPT Press, 2016). And outlining what it might mean to pursue a literary reading further—especially one informed by current Americanist scholarship—is **Elizabeth Fenton and Jared Hickman, eds.,** *Americanist Approaches to "The Book of Mormon"* (New York: Oxford University Press, 2019).

PART 3: GETTING SPECIALIZED

Once you've developed a sense for the field as a whole, you might be interested in pursuing a more specialized dimension of Book of Mormon studies. Because this field is small by comparison with many academic disciplines, some might feel like it's possible to become familiar with everything of importance in relatively short order. Others will certainly feel as if it's impossible to ever get to the bottom of so much research. Either way, it's crucial to recognize that there's often far more important past scholarship to be surveyed than is expected when it comes to more specific topics in Book of Mormon studies. And these specialist literatures are far too often ignored by students working their way into the field. Here in part 3, then, we introduce resources mentioned or alluded to in the preceding pages that will be of particular interest to students of the Book of Mormon hoping to get more specific.

Students of the Book of Mormon interested in the textual history of the Book of Mormon beyond the resources appearing in part 2 should see *The Joseph Smith Papers* editions of the original and printer's manuscripts of the Book of Mormon: **Royal Skousen and Robin Scott Jensen, eds., *Revelations and Translations, Volume 3: Printer's Manuscript of the Book of Mormon*,** facsimile ed., 2 pts., vol. 3 of the Revelations and Translations series of *The Joseph Smith Papers*, ed. Ronald K. Esplin and Matthew J. Grow (Salt Lake City: Church Historian's Press, 2015); and **Royal Skousen and Robin Scott Jensen, eds., *Revelations and Translations, Volume 5: Original Manuscript of the Book of Mormon*,** facsimile ed., vol. 5 of the Revelations and Translations series of *The Joseph Smith Papers*, ed. Matthew C. Godfrey, R. Eric Smith, Matthew J. Grow, and Ronald K. Esplin (Salt Lake City: Church Historian's Press, 2021). Also essential is **Royal Skousen, *The History of the Text of the Book of Mormon*,** 7 vols. (Provo, UT: FARMS; BYU Studies, 2016–21). For an important early effort to produce a critical text of the Book of Mormon, see **Robert F. Smith, ed., *Book of Mormon Critical Text: A Tool for Scholarly Reference*, 3 vols.** (Provo, UT: FARMS, 1984).

In addition to works already mentioned on the translation and publication of the Book of Mormon, interested students should be familiar with the more detailed history recounted in **Richard L. Bushman, *Joseph Smith and the Beginnings of Mormonism*** (Urbana: University of Illinois Press, 1984). Historical sources can be found compiled in **Larry E. Morris, ed., *A Documentary History of the Book of Mormon*** (New York: Oxford University Press, 2019). Hugh Nibley's response to Fawn Brodie's infamous biography of Joseph Smith is titled **"No, Ma'am, That's Not History: A Brief Review of Mrs. Brodie's Reluctant Vindication of a Prophet She Seeks to Expose,"** in *The Collected Works of Hugh Nibley*, vol. 11, *Tinkling Cymbals and Sounding Brass*, ed. David J. Whittaker (Provo, UT: FARMS; Salt Lake City, UT: Deseret Book, 1991), 1–45. An important but problematic development of D. Michael Quinn's work on these issues is **John L. Brooke, *The Refiner's Fire: The Making of Mormon Cosmology, 1644–1844*** (New York: Cambridge University Press, 1994). For Brant Gardner's development of Blake Ostler's expansion theory of the Book of Mormon, see **Brant A. Gardner, *The Gift and Power: Translating the Book of Mormon*** (Salt Lake City: Greg Kofford Books, 2011). For more recent work on the textual history of the Book of Mormon, see especially **William L. Davis, *Visions in a Seer Stone:***

Appendix

Joseph Smith and the Making of the Book of Mormon (Chapel Hill: University of North Carolina Press, 2020); and **Samuel Morris Brown,** *Joseph Smith's Translation: The Words and Worlds of Early Mormonism* (New York: Oxford University Press, 2020).

Students of the Book of Mormon interested in the defense of the historicity of the Book of Mormon should be familiar with **Sidney B. Sperry,** *The Book of Mormon Testifies* (Salt Lake City: Bookcraft, 1952); and **Sidney B. Sperry,** *The Problems of the Book of Mormon* (Salt Lake City: Bookcraft, 1964). (The latter was later published in 1967 under the title *Answers to Book of Mormon Questions*.) Some of the most important among Sperry's contributions were gathered in a special issue of the *Journal of Book of Mormon Studies*: volume 4, issue 1 (1995). Obviously crucial also is Hugh Nibley, and among Nibley's key works on the Book of Mormon as yet unmentioned are *Lehi in the Desert / The World of the Jaredites / There Were Jaredites*, vol. 5 of *The Collected Works of Hugh Nibley* (Provo, UT: FARMS; Salt Lake City, UT: Deseret Book, 1988); *An Approach to the Book of Mormon*, 3rd ed., vol. 6 of *The Collected Works of Hugh Nibley* (Provo, UT: FARMS; Salt Lake City, UT: Deseret Book, 1988); and the essays gathered in *The Prophetic Book of Mormon*, vol. 8 of *The Collected Works of Hugh Nibley* (Provo, UT: FARMS; Salt Lake City, UT: Deseret Book, 1989).

Key works by FARMS scholars not mentioned in part 2 include the essential stand-alone books by founder John Welch: *The Sermon at the Temple and the Sermon on the Mount: A Latter-day Saint Approach* (Provo, UT: FARMS; Salt Lake City, UT: Deseret Book, 1990); and *The Legal Cases in the Book of Mormon* (Provo, UT: BYU Studies; Neal A. Maxwell Institute for Religious Scholarship, 2008). Also, previously unmentioned FARMS volumes of particular value and importance are **Donald W. Parry and John W. Welch, eds.,** *Isaiah in the Book of Mormon* (Provo, UT: FARMS, 1998); **Noel B. Reynolds, ed.,** *Book of Mormon Authorship Revisited: The Evidence for Ancient Origins* (Provo, UT: FARMS, 1997); and **John W. Welch, David Rolph Seely, and Jo Ann H. Seely, eds.,** *Glimpses of Lehi's Jerusalem* (Provo, UT: FARMS, 2004). See also **Andrew C. Skinner and Gaye Strathearn, eds.,** *Third Nephi: An Incomparable Scripture* (Provo, UT: Neal A. Maxwell Institute for Religious Scholarship; Salt Lake City, UT: Deseret Book, 2012).

Critical responses to FARMS scholarship (and some of its predecessors) appear famously and most importantly in **Brent Lee Metcalfe, ed.,** *New Approaches to the Book of Mormon: Explorations in Critical Methodology* (Salt Lake City: Signature Books, 1993). FARMS scholars responded to this book in numerous reviews and essays, especially in volume 6, issue 1 (1994), of the *Review of Books on the Book of Mormon*. The important acknowledgment of FARMS's scholarship from evangelical scholars can be found in **Carl Mosser and Paul Owen, "Mormon Scholarship, Apologetics, and Evangelical Neglect: Losing the Battle and Not Knowing It?,"** *Trinity Journal* 19, no. 2 (Fall 1998): 179–205. Responding to their own essay, Mosser and Owen gathered further critical responses to FARMS scholarship in **Francis J. Beckwith, Carl Mosser, and Paul Owen, eds.,** *The New Mormon Challenge: Responding to the Latest Defenses of a Fast-Growing Movement* (Grand Rapids, MI: Zondervan, 2002). For helpful theoretical reflections on the nature of apologetics, see **Blair G. Van Dyke and Loyd Isao Ericson, eds.,** *Perspectives on Mormon Theology: Apologetics* (Salt Lake City: Greg Kofford Books, 2017).

Those interested in Book of Mormon geography can find a good summary of what's been done in **Andrew H. Hedges, "Book of Mormon Geographies,"** *BYU Studies Quarterly* 60, no. 3 (2021): 193–202. They should be especially familiar with the writings of John Sorenson. Beyond what's already mentioned in part 2 are **John L. Sorenson,** *Mormon's Codex: An Ancient American Book* (Provo, UT: Neal A. Maxwell Institute for Religious Scholarship; Salt Lake City, UT: Deseret Book, 2013); and the especially helpful reference volumes **John L. Sorenson,** *The Geography of Book of Mormon Events: A Source Book* (Provo, UT: FARMS, 1992); and **John L. Sorenson,** *Mormon's Map* (Provo, UT: FARMS, 2000).

The most important of Brant Gardner's conclusions in his commentary *Second Witness* have been gathered into a sustained treatment in **Brant A. Gardner,** *Traditions of the Fathers: The Book of Mormon as History* (Salt Lake City: Greg Kofford Books, 2015). Good examinations of particular issues representing a new generation of Mesoamericanists are **Mark Alan Wright, "Joseph Smith and Native American Artifacts,"** in *Approaching Antiquity: Joseph Smith and the Ancient World*, ed.

Lincoln H. Blumell, Matthew J. Grey, and Andrew H. Hedges (Provo, UT: Religious Studies Center, Brigham Young University; Salt Lake City, UT: Deseret Book, 2015), 119–40; and **Kerry Hull, "An 'East Wind': Old and New World Perspectives,"** in *Abinadi: He Came among Them in Disguise*, ed. Shon D. Hopkin (Provo, UT: Religious Studies Center, Brigham Young University; Salt Lake City, UT: Deseret Book, 2018), 169–208. For important critiques of the Mesoamerican model, see **Deanne G. Matheny, "Does the Shoe Fit? A Critique of the Limited Tehuantepec Geography,"** in *New Approaches to the Book of Mormon: Explorations in Critical Methodology*, ed. Brent Lee Metcalfe (Salt Lake City: Signature Books, 1993), 269–328.

Key representative works from those promoting a Heartland model (the model that assumes that the events of the Book of Mormon took place geographically within the United States) are **Rod L. Meldrum, *Exploring the Book of Mormon in America's Heartland: A Visual Journey of Discovery*** (New York: Digital Legend Press, 2011); and **Bruce H. Porter and Rod L. Meldrum, *Prophecies and Promises: The Book of Mormon and the United States of America*** (New York: Digital Legend Press, 2009). Important responses to the Heartland project are **Mark Alan Wright, "Heartland as Hinterland: The Mesoamerican Core and North American Periphery of Book of Mormon Geography,"** *Interpreter: A Journal of Mormon Scripture* 13 (2015): 111–29; and **Gregory L. Smith, "Often in Error, Seldom in Doubt: Rod Meldrum and Book of Mormon DNA,"** *FARMS Review* 22, no. 1 (2010): 17–161.

Recent years have seen the emergence of a handful of Book of Mormon scholars interested in pressing forward with setting the book in its ancient context but without making *arguing* for historicity central to their work. Such studies are helpfully illuminating the text for a believing readership without becoming embroiled in debates. Particularly helpful starting points for seeing what this scholarship looks like are **Daniel Belnap, "'And It Came to Pass . . .': The Sociopolitical Events in the Book of Mormon Leading to the Eighteenth Year of the Reign of the Judges,"** *Journal of Book of Mormon Studies* 23 (2014): 101–39; **Daniel Belnap, "'And He Was Anti-Christ': The Significance of the Eighteenth Year of the Reign of the Judges, Part 2,"** *Journal of Book of Mormon Studies* 28 (2019): 91–136; and **Avram R. Shannon, "Law of God/God** of Law: The Law of Moses in Alma's Teachings to Corianton," in *Give Ear to My Words: Text and Context of Alma 36–42*, ed. Kerry M. Hull, Nicholas J. Frederick, and Hank R. Smith (Provo, UT: Religious Studies Center, Brigham Young University; Salt Lake City, UT: Deseret Book, 2019), 129–54.

Major works from the doctrinal school of interpretation, especially prominent during the 1980s and 1990s, include those in the **Book of Mormon Symposium series**, 9 vols. (Provo, UT: Religious Studies Center, Brigham Young University, 1988–94). Also important have been volumes of essays given at the annual BYU Sidney B. Sperry Symposium, which focuses on the Book of Mormon every four years. See especially important volumes in more recent years: **Daniel L. Belnap, Gaye Strathearn, and Stanley A. Johnson, eds.,** *The Things Which My Father Saw: Approaches to Lehi's Dream and Nephi's Vision* (Provo, UT: Religious Studies Center, Brigham Young University; Salt Lake City, UT: Deseret Book, 2011); **Dennis L. Largey, Andrew H. Hedges, John Hilton III, and Kerry Hull, eds.,** *The Coming Forth of the Book of Mormon: A Marvelous Work and a Wonder* (Provo, UT: Religious Studies Center, Brigham Young University; Salt Lake City, UT: Deseret Book, 2015); and **Kerry M. Hull, Nicholas J. Frederick, and Hank R. Smith,** *Give Ear to My Words: Text and Context of Alma 36–42* (Provo, UT: Religious Studies Center, Brigham Young University; Salt Lake City, UT: Deseret Book, 2019). For the most important doctrinal reading of the whole of the Book of Mormon, see **Joseph Fielding McConkie, Robert L. Millet, and Brent L. Top,** *Doctrinal Commentary on the Book of Mormon*, 4 vols. (Salt Lake City: Bookcraft, 1987–92). See also, however, the important critique of this work by **Louis Midgley,** "**Prophetic Messages or Dogmatic Theology? Commenting on the Book of Mormon: A Review Essay,**" *Review of Books on the Book of Mormon* 1, no. 1 (1989): 92–113.

Literary students of the Book of Mormon should be familiar with the earliest fruits of literary work on the volume, published in the early 1980s. Especially important are *Proceedings of the Association for Mormon Letters, 1979–82* (Salt Lake City: Association for Mormon Letters, 1983); and **Neal E. Lambert, ed.,** *Literature of Belief: Sacred Scripture and Religious Experience* (Provo, UT: Religious Studies

Center, Brigham Young University, 1981). Late 1990s flowerings of some of this early work include **Richard Dilworth Rust,** *Feasting on the Word: The Literary Testimony of the Book of Mormon* (Provo, UT: FARMS; Salt Lake City, UT: Deseret Book, 1997); **Marilyn Arnold,** *Sweet Is the Word: Reflections on the Book of Mormon—Its Narrative, Teachings, and People* (American Fork, UT: Covenant Communications, 1996); and **Mark D. Thomas,** *Digging in Cumorah: Reclaiming Book of Mormon Narratives* (Salt Lake City: Signature Books, 1999). Grant Hardy provided a particularly important review of Thomas's book in **"Speaking So That All May Be Edified,"** *FARMS Review of Books* 12, no. 2 (2000): 83–97.

As for the twenty-first century, Amy Easton-Flake has provided a valuable review of Grant Hardy's seminal work, along with a detailed outline of narratology in **"Beyond Understanding: Narrative Theory as Expansion in Book of Mormon Exegesis,"** *Journal of Book of Mormon Studies* 25, no. 1 (2016): 116–38. More recent works push literary study into the field of Americanism and address the place of the Book of Mormon in American literature. Especially important here, besides works mentioned in part 2, are **Peter Coviello,** *Make Yourselves Gods: Mormons and the Unfinished Business of American Secularism* (Chicago: University of Chicago Press, 2019); **Elizabeth Fenton,** *Old Canaan in a New World: Native Americans and the Lost Tribes of Israel* (New York: New York University Press, 2020); **David F. Holland,** *Sacred Borders: Continuing Revelation and Canonical Restraint in Early America* (New York: Oxford University Press, 2011); **Seth Perry,** *Bible Culture and Authority in the Early United States* (Princeton: Princeton University Press, 2018); and **Eran Shalev,** *American Zion: The Old Testament as a Political Text from the Revolution to the Civil War* (New Haven: Yale University Press, 2013). See also **Elizabeth Fenton, "Open Canons: Sacred History and American History in *The Book of Mormon*,"** *J19: The Journal of Nineteenth-Century Americanists* 1, no. 2 (Fall 2013): 339–61. For texts contemporary with the publication of the Book of Mormon that are often commented on, see **Kent P. Jackson, ed.,** *Manuscript Found: The Complete Original "Spaulding Manuscript"* (Provo, UT: Religious Studies Center, Brigham Young University, 1996);

and **Charles D. Tate Jr., ed., *View of the Hebrews: 1825 Second Edition*** (Provo, UT: Religious Studies Center, Brigham Young University, 1996).

For students interested in developments in Book of Mormon studies that reflect larger trends in the world of biblical scholarship, it might be best to begin with a guide to methods in biblical studies, such as **John H. Hayes and Carl R. Holladay, *Biblical Exegesis: A Beginner's Handbook***, 3rd ed. (Louisville: Westminster John Knox Press, 2007). Genre-defining treatments of intertextuality and reception history, less represented in handbooks for interpretation, include **Richard B. Hays, *Echoes of Scripture in the Letters of Paul*** (New Haven: Yale University Press, 1989); and **John F. A. Sawyer, *The Fifth Gospel: Isaiah in the History of Christianity*** (New York: Cambridge University Press, 1996). A helpful primer on scriptural theology can be found in **James K. Mead, *Biblical Theology: Issues, Methods, and Themes*** (Louisville: Westminster John Knox Press, 2007).

Major works on the Book of Mormon's reception appear in part 1 and part 2 of this appendix. An important edition of the Book of Mormon (using the 1840 edition), however, comes with a contextual introduction to the book's reception: **Laurie F. Maffly-Kipp, ed., *The Book of Mormon*** (New York: Penguin, 2008). The early commentary by Reynolds and Sjödahl represents interpretation of the Book of Mormon on the eve of Book of Mormon studies: **George Reynolds and Janne M. Sjödahl, *Commentary on the Book of Mormon***, ed. Philip C. Reynolds, 7 vols. (Salt Lake City: Deseret Book, 1955). Another important contribution to reception history, although from an idiosyncratic position, is **Daymon M. Smith, *A Cultural History of the Book of Mormon***, 8 vols. (n.p.: self-published, 2013–14).

Important works on connections between the Book of Mormon and the Bible stretch back into the twentieth century, with long-standing treatments appearing in Sidney Sperry's *Answers to Book of Mormon Questions* and Hugh Nibley's *Since Cumorah*. Approaches similar to those of Sperry and Nibley are reflected well in **Kent P. Jackson, "Isaiah in the Book of Mormon,"** in *A Reason for Faith: Navigating LDS Doctrine and Church History*, ed. Laura Harris Hales (Provo, UT: Religious Studies Center, Brigham Young University; Salt Lake City, UT: Deseret Book, 2016), 69–78. More recent work, however, on the important issue of quotations from Isaiah in the Book of Mormon includes **Joseph M. Spencer**, *The Vision of All: Twenty-Five Lectures on Isaiah in Nephi's Record* (Salt Lake City: Greg Kofford Books, 2016). On the New Testament's relationship to the Book of Mormon, beyond his book mentioned in part 2 (*The Bible, Mormon Scripture, and the Rhetoric of Allusivity*), see **Nicholas J. Frederick**, "Evaluating the Interaction between the New Testament and the Book of Mormon: A Proposed Methodology," *Journal of Book of Mormon Studies* 24 (2015): 1–30; **Nicholas J. Frederick**, "The Book of Mormon and Its Redaction of the King James New Testament: A Further Evaluation of the Interaction between the New Testament and the Book of Mormon," *Journal of Book of Mormon Studies* 27 (2018): 44–87; and **Nicholas J. Frederick**, "Finding Meaning(s) in How the Book of Mormon Uses the New Testament," *Journal of Book of Mormon Studies* 30 (2021): 1–35.

Preliminary studies of the Book of Mormon and other world scripture include—beyond Jad Hatem's *Postponing Heaven*, mentioned in part 2—**Grant Hardy**, "The Book of Mormon as Post-Canonical Scripture," in *The Expanded Canon: Perspectives on Mormonism and Sacred Texts*, ed. Blair G. Van Dyke, Brian D. Birch, and Boyd J. Petersen (Salt Lake City: Greg Kofford Books, 2018), 73–84; **Joseph M. Spencer**, "Christ and Krishna: The Visions of Arjuna and the Brother of Jared," *Journal of Book of Mormon Studies* 23 (2014): 56–80; and **D. Morgan Davis**, "Prophets and Prophecy in the Qur'an and the Book of Mormon," *Journal of Book of Mormon Studies* 29 (2020): 50–84.

An important summary treatment of how the Book of Mormon can speak to the marginalized is **Fatimah Salleh and Margaret Olsen Hemming**, *The Book of Mormon for the Least of These*, vol. 1, *1 Nephi–Words of Mormon* (Salt Lake City: By Common Consent Press, 2020). More specialized work speaking to disabilities in particular is **Blair Dee Hodges**, "A Disability Studies Reading of Moroni Chapter 8," *Journal of Book of Mormon Studies* 29 (2020): 309–22. Political issues, particularly with an emphasis on war (and violence) and peace, were already the subject of Hugh Nibley's studies in the last part of *Since Cumorah*, and important contributions came later in the twentieth century in **Lisa Bolin Hawkins and Gordon C. Thomasson**, "I Only Am Escaped to Tell Thee: Survivor Witnesses in the Book of Mormon," FARMS

Preliminary Report, 1984; **Gordon C. Thomasson**, "Mosiah: The Complex Symbolism and Symbolic Complex of Kingship in the Book of Mormon," *Journal of Book of Mormon Studies* 2, no. 1 (1993): 21–38; and **Eugene England**, "Why Nephi Killed Laban: Reflections on the Truth of the Book of Mormon," in *Making Peace: Personal Essays* (Salt Lake City: Signature Books, 1995), 131–56. Historical assessments of war in the Book of Mormon can be found in **Stephen D. Ricks and William J. Hamblin, eds.**, *Warfare in the Book of Mormon* (Provo, UT: FARMS, 1990). Representative works pointing the way in the twenty-first century are **David Charles Gore**, *The Voice of the People: Political Rhetoric in the Book of Mormon* (Provo, UT: Neal A. Maxwell Institute for Religious Scholarship, 2019); and **Patrick Q. Mason and J. David Pulsipher**, *Proclaim Peace: The Restoration's Answer to an Age of Conflict* (Provo, UT: Neal A. Maxwell Institute for Religious Scholarship; Salt Lake City, UT: Deseret Book, 2021).

For students interested in race and the Book of Mormon, it's necessary to add to the works cited already in part 2 the historical treatment by John Sorenson in *An Ancient American Setting for the Book of Mormon*, as well as **Eugene England**, "'Lamanites' and the Spirit of the Lord," *Dialogue: A Journal of Mormon Thought* 18, no. 4 (Winter 1985): 25–32. A novel and important proposal regarding race appears in **Ethan Sproat**, "Skins as Garments in the Book of Mormon: A Textual Exegesis," *Journal of Book of Mormon Studies* 24 (2015): 138–65. Crucial recent work includes especially **Max Perry Mueller**, *Race and the Making of the Mormon People* (Chapel Hill: University of North Carolina Press, 2017); and the summary essay **David M. Belnap**, "The Inclusive, Anti-Discrimination Message of the Book of Mormon," *Interpreter: A Journal of Latter-day Saint Faith and Scholarship* 42 (2021): 195–370.

For gender issues and the role of women in the Book of Mormon, see relatively conservative approaches from the late twentieth century in **Jerrie W. Hurd**, *Our Sisters in the Latter-Day Scriptures* (Salt Lake City: Deseret Book, 1987); **Francine R. Bennion**, "Women and the Book of Mormon: Tradition and Revelation," in *Women of Wisdom and Knowledge: Talks Selected from the BYU Women's Conferences*, ed. Marie Cornwall and Susan Howe (Salt Lake City: Deseret Book,

1990), 169–78; and **Camille S. Williams, "Women in the Book of Mormon: Inclusion, Exclusion, and Interpretation,"** *Journal of Book of Mormon Studies* 11, no. 1 (2002): 66–79, 111–14. For more obviously liberal positions from the same time period, see **Carol Lynn Pearson, "Could Feminism Have Saved the Nephites?,"** *Sunstone* 19, no. 1 (March 1996): 32–40; and **Lynn Matthews Anderson, "Toward a Feminist Interpretation of Latter-Day Scripture,"** *Dialogue: A Journal of Mormon Thought* 27, no. 2 (1994): 185–203. Essential recent work that's more informed by recent theory includes **Amy Easton-Flake, "Arise from the Dust, My Sons, and Be Men,"** in *Americanist Approaches to "The Book of Mormon,"* ed. Elizabeth Fenton and Jared Hickman (New York: Oxford University Press, 2019), 362–90; **Kimberly Matheson Berkey and Joseph M. Spencer, "'Great Cause to Mourn': The Complexity of *The Book of Mormon*'s Presentation of Gender and Race,"** in *Americanist Approaches to "The Book of Mormon,"* 298–320; and **Deidre Nicole Green,** *Jacob: A Brief Theological Introduction* (Provo, UT: Neal A. Maxwell Institute for Religious Scholarship, 2020). For a recent survey of gender in the Book of Mormon without a particular theoretical angle, see **Heather Farrell and Mandy Jane Williams,** *Walking with the Women of the Book of Mormon* (Springville, UT: Cedar Fort, 2019).

The theological approach to the Book of Mormon can be studied especially by surveying volumes published by the Latter-day Saint Theology Seminar. To date, see **Adam S. Miller, ed.,** *An Experiment on the Word: Reading Alma 32* (Provo, UT: Neal A. Maxwell Institute for Religious Scholarship, 2014); **Joseph M. Spencer and Jenny Webb, eds.,** *Reading Nephi Reading Isaiah: 2 Nephi 26–27* (Provo, UT: Neal A. Maxwell Institute for Religious Scholarship, 2016); **Adam S. Miller, ed.,** *A Dream, a Rock, and a Pillar of Fire: Reading 1 Nephi 1* (Provo, UT: Neal A. Maxwell Institute for Religious Scholarship, 2017); **Adam S. Miller and Joseph M. Spencer, eds.,** *Christ and Antichrist: Reading Jacob 7* (Provo, UT: Neal A. Maxwell Institute for Religious Scholarship, 2017); and **Matthew Bowman and Rosemary Demos, eds.,** *A Preparatory Redemption: Reading Alma 12–13* (Provo, UT: Neal A. Maxwell Institute for Religious Scholarship, 2018).

Appendix

PART 4: GETTING AROUND

In addition to books and essays on the Book of Mormon, there are naturally many institutions sponsoring and publishing work on the Book of Mormon. It's important to be aware of what and where these institutions are. Some host conferences and symposia, some publish essays or books, and some gather and archive material online. Beyond getting familiar with the larger field and a specialized subdiscipline, it's useful to know where to turn either to find good work on the Book of Mormon or to take one's own work for institutional support or potential publication. Here we outline the shape of the various institutions operating within the field of Book of Mormon studies.

Since its first appearance in 1992, the premier scholarly journal for the field has been the *Journal of Book of Mormon Studies*. From the beginning, the journal has been devoted to publishing a wide range of Book of Mormon scholarship, representing informed amateur scholarship as well as scholarship produced by established scholars. It's currently published once a year and includes research articles, book reviews, reviews of literature, short research notes, and an annual bibliography—in addition to occasional special features (such as roundtable discussions or interviews).

Several other journals regularly publish work on the Book of Mormon. *BYU Studies Quarterly* publishes occasional work on the Book of Mormon addressed to an educated Latter-day Saint readership. The *Religious Educator: Perspectives on the Restored Gospel*, published by BYU's Religious Studies Center (see below), regularly publishes studies of the Book of Mormon, principally with a focus on material that might be useful for those who teach the Book of Mormon in the classroom. The *Interpreter: A Journal of Latter-day Saint Faith and Scholarship* publishes a good deal of scholarship on the Book of Mormon, most of it in the vein of traditional twentieth-century scholarship. Historical studies of reception of or the coming forth of the Book of Mormon occasionally appear in *Latter-day Saint Historical Studies* (formerly *Mormon Historical Studies*) and the *Journal of Mormon History*. Two periodicals that are more controversial, *Dialogue: A Journal of Mormon Thought* and *Sunstone*, have published important work on the Book of Mormon and occasionally publish such work today. These journals publish work from an informed and often academic perspective, even if sometimes from a point of view that troubles traditional believers.

And of course, studies of the Book of Mormon can be found scattered across the publishing world in various scholarly journals in addition to the ones discussed here. Those articles can be best found using online databases such as EBSCO or Google Scholar. The annual bibliography in the *Journal of Book of Mormon Studies* attempts to discover and list all these further-flung publications each year.

Various outfits publish full book-length studies of the Book of Mormon. By far the most important of these historically was the Foundation for Ancient Research and Mormon Studies (FARMS), which published dozens of books on the Book of Mormon—as well as the *Journal of Book of Mormon Studies* and the *FARMS Review* in its various iterations—during the 1980s and 1990s. The Neal A. Maxwell Institute for Religious Scholarship (see below) took responsibility for FARMS's operations in 2006 and has continued publishing book-length studies of the Book of Mormon, as well as the *Journal of Book of Mormon Studies*. While FARMS specialized in treatments of the Book of Mormon arguing for its ancient historicity (whether through an ancient American setting or through connections with the ancient Near East), the Maxwell Institute has especially privileged theological work on the Book of Mormon. It accordingly has published not only the multivolume **Book of Mormon: Brief Theological Introductions** and the proceedings of the Latter-day Saint Theology Seminar (see below) but also the **Groundwork: Studies in Theory and Scripture** series. The Interpreter Foundation, publisher of the *Interpreter* (mentioned above), publishes occasional books in the traditional FARMS vein. All these principally aim to speak to educated Latter-day Saints.

BYU's Religious Studies Center (RSC) often publishes scholarly work on the Book of Mormon, generally in collaboration with Deseret Book (see below) and also always with the aim of reaching educated Latter-day Saints. It publishes, for instance, the proceedings of the Sidney B. Sperry Symposium, held at BYU every year and focused on the Book of Mormon every fourth year. The Religious Studies Center also publishes volumes assembled by BYU's Book of Mormon Academy (see below), such as volumes on Abinadi (in 2018), the Jaredites (in

2019), Samuel the Lamanite (in 2021), and the Bible's relationship with the Book of Mormon (in 2022). Apart from these series of sorts, the RSC occasionally publishes stand-alone volumes on the Book of Mormon. Deseret Book, the primary publishing outlet for The Church of Jesus Christ of Latter-day Saints, frequently publishes content on the Book of Mormon but primarily from a devotional perspective.

A major publisher of work on the Book of Mormon, more scholarly in tone than but often just as confessional as more traditional publishers, is Greg Kofford Books. Important as an independent publishing outfit, it has published some of the most important Book of Mormon scholarship in the twenty-first century, opening its doors with Boyd Jay Petersen's biography of Hugh Nibley (*Hugh Nibley: A Consecrated Life*) and then publishing a few years later Brant Gardner's crucial six-volume commentary, *Second Witness*. Also independent but much more partisan is Signature Books, often the avowed publishing rival to FARMS during the 1980s and 1990s. Signature published much work of a critical nature during its heyday, as well as more decidedly neutral and even confessionally traditional works. It has published relatively little on the Book of Mormon during the twenty-first century.

Various traditional academic presses have become interested in publishing work on the Book of Mormon in the past two decades. Particularly important among these are two publishers with strong commitments to work on the Latter-day Saint tradition: Oxford University Press (the publisher of Terryl Givens's *By the Hand of Mormon*, Grant Hardy's *Understanding the Book of Mormon*, and Elizabeth Fenton and Jared Hickman's *Americanist Approaches to "The Book of Mormon"*) and the University of Illinois Press (the publisher of Grant Hardy's *The Book of Mormon: A Reader's Edition* and, with the Maxwell Institute, the *Journal of Book of Mormon Studies*). Additional major publications have appeared from Yale University Press, Princeton University Press, the University of North Carolina Press, the University of Chicago Press, and Fairleigh Dickinson University Press. Many major academic presses are interested in publishing solid scholarly work on the Book of Mormon that has a broader appeal.

Several websites gather much good information about the Book of Mormon or archive past Book of Mormon scholarship so that it's readily accessible. The most important of these is unquestionably Book of Mormon Central (bookofmormoncentral.org), which archives astonishing amounts of past Book of Mormon scholarship on its website. Beyond archiving past work, Book of Mormon Central creates online media about the Book of Mormon, especially focusing on establishing the historicity of the text, and provides resources for everyday readers of the Book of Mormon interested in deeper study. It has also begun to publish some of its popularizing work, especially in the Knowing Why series. Another important online resource is the Foundation for Apologetic Information and Research (FAIR) website (fairlatterdaysaints.org), which provides well-documented answers to difficult questions and issues surrounding the text of the Book of Mormon—often drawing on the work of FARMS scholars. A more specialized online resource is the Book of Mormon Onomasticon (onoma.lib.byu.edu), which gathers information on potential meanings for Book of Mormon names in light of ancient languages.

Four institutions lead the way in promoting current and ongoing Book of Mormon research in a focused way. In 2017, a conference held in Logan, Utah, devoted toward furthering serious study of the Book of Mormon, led to the creation of the Book of Mormon Studies Association. Aimed at both Latter-day Saint and non–Latter-day Saint scholars of the Book of Mormon, the organization holds annual conferences (at Utah State University) aimed at establishing a space for serious discussion of the Book of Mormon. The association does not sponsor any publication directly, encouraging conference participants to pursue publication of their work in established journals and other publication outfits. The organization welcomes major scholars as keynote speakers each year and features dozens of papers from current researchers in the field.

The Maxwell Institute, in addition to publishing work on the Book of Mormon, actively promotes Book of Mormon scholarship through conferences, seminars, and other events. Since 2014, it has helped sponsor annual seminars held by the Latter-day Saint Theology Seminar (see below), and it has held occasional symposia on Book of Mormon topics since its creation in 2006. It hosts in-person and online events about Book of Mormon scholarship and occasionally features Book of Mormon scholars on the Maxwell Institute Podcast. In addition, the Maxwell Institute sponsors postdoctoral positions specifically for scholars seriously producing scholarship on the Book of Mormon. Finally, every other year the Maxwell Institute hosts the Laura F. Willes Lecture on the Book of Mormon, a talk that is then published. Speakers have included John Welch, James Faulconer, Terryl Givens, and David Holland, among others.

The Book of Mormon Academy, founded in 2013 as part of the Department of Ancient Scripture at BYU, consists of several of the department's faculty members who devote part of their research to the Book of Mormon. Although the academy sponsors a variety of minor initiatives, including efforts to improve teaching on the Book of Mormon and efforts to reach out to lay Latter-day Saints, its primary mark in Book of Mormon scholarship is a series of studies of shorter stretches of the Book of Mormon. Published by the Religious Studies Center, the series so far has volumes on Abinadi, the Jaredites, and Samuel the Lamanite, with other volumes currently under construction. Written from the perspective of faith, these volumes work to promote much closer reading of particular passages in the Book of Mormon than has appeared in previous scholarship, and they are informed by a variety of disciplinary backgrounds.

Begun in 2008, the Latter-day Saint Theology Seminar (originally the Mormon Theology Seminar) has hosted numerous in-depth seminars on single chapters of the Book of Mormon. Originally hosting online seminars followed by public in-person symposia, it has since 2014 held annual in-person seminars in collaboration with the Maxwell Institute and a variety of other academic institutions. Each seminar gathers six to ten scholars with various backgrounds to work in a theological and literary way on short texts from scripture—generally from the Book of Mormon. At the end of each intensive seminar, participants produce individual papers, and the seminarians collectively produce a report of their shared findings. The proceedings then appear in print. Volumes on Alma 32; 2 Nephi 26–27; 1 Nephi 1; Jacob 7; Alma 12–13; and Mosiah 15 have appeared to date, and other volumes are in production.

Appendix

PART 5: OTHER SOURCES WE'VE CITED ALONG THE WAY

Austin, Michael. "How the Book of Mormon Reads the Bible: A Theory of Types." *Journal of Book of Mormon Studies* 26 (2017): 48–81.

Benson, Ezra Taft. *A Witness and a Warning: A Modern-Day Prophet Testifies of the Book of Mormon*. Salt Lake City: Deseret Book, 1988.

Berkey, Kimberly M. "Temporality and Fulfillment in 3 Nephi 1." *Journal of Book of Mormon Studies* 24, no. 1 (2015): 53–83.

Berrett, William E., Milton R. Hunter, Roy A. Welker, and H. Alvah Fitzgerald. *A Guide to the Study of the Book of Mormon*. Salt Lake City: Department of Education of The Church of Jesus Christ of Latter-day Saints, 1938.

Blythe, Christopher James. "'A Very Fine Azteck Manuscript': Latter-day Saint Readings of Codex Boturini." *Journal of Book of Mormon Studies* 26 (2017): 185–217.

"Book of Mormon Geography." Gospel Topics. ChurchofJesusChrist.org.

Boxer, Elise. "The Book of Mormon as Mormon Settler Colonialism." In *Essays on American Indian and Mormon History*, edited by P. Jane Hafen and Brenden W. Rensink, 3–22. Salt Lake City: University of Utah Press, 2019.

Compton, Todd M. "The Spirituality of the Outcast in the Book of Mormon." *Journal of Book of Mormon Studies* 2, no. 1 (1993): 139–60.

Erdmann, Angela. "Subjective Objects: 'The Book of Pukei' and Early Critical Response to *The Book of Mormon*." *Journal of Book of Mormon Studies* 27 (2018): 163–74.

Fenton, Elizabeth, and Joseph M. Spencer. "Teaching *The Book of Mormon* at the University of Vermont: An Interview with Elizabeth Fenton by Joseph Spencer." *Journal of Book of Mormon Studies* 27 (2018): 128–48.

Frederick, Nicholas J., and Joseph M. Spencer. "The Book of Mormon and the Academy." *Religious Educator* 21, no. 2 (2020): 171–92.

———. "John 11 in the Book of Mormon." *Journal of the Bible and Its Reception* 5, no. 1 (2018): 81–106.

Frye, Northrop. *Anatomy of Criticism: Four Essays*. Princeton: Princeton University Press, 1957.

Hickman, Jared. "*The Book of Mormon* as Amerindian Apocalypse." *American Literature* 86, no. 3 (2014): 429–61.

Hunt, Gilbert J. *The Late War, between the United States and Great Britain, from June, 1812, to February, 1815*. New York: Daniel D. Smith, 1819.

Hutchinson, Anthony A. "The Word of God Is Enough: The Book of Mormon as Nineteenth-Century Scripture." In *New Approaches to the Book of Mormon: Explorations in Critical Methodology*, edited by Brent Lee Metcalfe, 1–19. Salt Lake City: Signature Books, 1993.

Jakeman, M. Wells. *The Complex "Tree-of-Life" Carving on Izapa Stela 5: A Reanalysis and Partial Interpretation*. Provo, UT: Brigham Young University, 1958.

———. *Stela 5, Izapa, Chiapas, Mexico: A Major Archaeological Discovery of the New World*. Provo, UT: Brigham Young University, 1958.

Jensen, Robin Scott. "Abner Cole and *The Reflector*: Another Clue to the Timing of the 1830 Book of Mormon Printing." *Journal of Book of Mormon Studies* 24 (2015): 238–47.

King, Farina. "Indigenizing Mormonisms." *Mormon Studies Review* 6 (2019): 1–16.

Madsen, Truman G. *Defender of the Faith: The B. H. Roberts Story*. Salt Lake City: Bookcraft, 1980.

Mauro, Hayes Peter. *Messianic Fulfillments: Staging Indigenous Salvation in America*. Lincoln: University of Nebraska Press, 2019.

Appendix

McConkie, Bruce R. *Doctrinal New Testament Commentary*. 3 vols. Salt Lake City: Bookcraft, 1965–73.

McConkie, Joseph Fielding, Robert L. Millet, and Brent L. Top. *Doctrinal Commentary on the Book of Mormon*. 4 vols. Salt Lake City: Bookcraft, 1987–92.

Midgley, Louis. "No Middle Ground: The Debate over the Authenticity of the Book of Mormon." In *Historicity and the Latter-day Saint Scriptures*, edited by Paul Y. Hoskisson, 149–70. Provo, UT: Religious Studies Center, Brigham Young University, 2001.

Miller, Adam S. "Messianic History: Walter Benjamin and the Book of Mormon." In *Rube Goldberg Machines: Essays in Mormon Theology*, 21–35. Salt Lake City: Greg Kofford Books, 2012.

Millet, Robert L. "The Book of Mormon, Historicity, and Faith." *Journal of Book of Mormon Studies* 2, no. 2 (1993): 1–13.

Mitchell, Samuel. "'Caught with Guile': Tricksters in the Book of Mormon." *Journal of Book of Mormon Studies* 29 (2020): 152–77.

Murphy, Thomas W. "Other Scriptures: Restoring Voices of Gantowisas to an Open Canon." In *Essays on American Indian and Mormon History*, edited by P. Jane Hafen and Brenden W. Rensink, 23–40. Salt Lake City: University of Utah Press, 2019.

Nibley, Hugh. *The Myth Makers*. Salt Lake City: Bookcraft, 1961.

———. "New Approaches to Book of Mormon Study." In *The Prophetic Book of Mormon*, 54–126. Vol. 8 of *The Collected Works of Hugh Nibley*. Provo, UT: FARMS; Salt Lake City, UT: Deseret Book, 1989.

———. *No, Ma'am, That's Not History: A Brief Review of Mrs. Brodie's Reluctant Vindication of a Prophet She Seeks to Expose*. Salt Lake City: Bookcraft, 1946.

Nyman, Monte S. *Book of Mormon Commentary*. 6 vols. Orem, UT: Granite, 2003.

Ogden, D. Kelly, and Andrew C. Skinner. *Verse by Verse: The Book of Mormon*. 2 vols. Salt Lake City: Deseret Book, 2011.

Pratt, Orson. *A[n] Interesting Account of Several Remarkable Visions, and of the Late Discovery of Ancient American Records*. Edinburgh: Ballantyne and Hughes, 1840.

Pulsipher, J. David. "Buried Swords: The Shifting Interpretive Ground of a Beloved Book of Mormon Narrative." *Journal of Book of Mormon Studies* 26 (2017): 1–47.

Rees, Robert A., and Eugene England, eds. *The Reader's Book of Mormon*. Salt Lake City: Signature Books, 2008.

Reynolds, George. *A Complete Concordance to the Book of Mormon*. Salt Lake City: self-published, 1900.

———. *A Dictionary of the Book of Mormon, Comprising Its Biographical, Geographical and Other Proper Names*. Salt Lake City: Joseph Hyrum Parry, 1891.

———. *The Story of the Book of Mormon*. Salt Lake City: Joseph Hyrum Parry, 1888.

Reynolds, Noel B. "Nephi's Outline." In *Book of Mormon Authorship: New Light on Ancient Origins*, edited by Noel B. Reynolds, 53–74. Provo, UT: Religious Studies Center, Brigham Young University, 1982.

Riess, Jana, ed. *The Book of Mormon: Selections Annotated and Explained*. Woodstock, VT: Skylight Paths, 2005.

Roberts, B. H. *A New Witness for God*. Salt Lake City: George Q. Cannon and Sons, 1895.

———. *Studies of the Book of Mormon*. Edited by Brigham D. Madsen. Urbana: University of Illinois Press, 1985.

———. "Translation of the Book of Mormon." *Improvement Era*, April 1906, 428–30.

Appendix

Robinson, Stephen E. "Review of *The Word of God: Essays on Mormon Scripture* by Dan Vogel." *FARMS Review of Books* 3, no. 1 (1991): 312–18.

Rosenvall, Lynn A., and David L. Rosenvall, eds. *A New Approach to Studying the Book of Mormon: Another Testament of Jesus Christ.* N.p.: Olive Leaf Foundation, 2017.

Sjödahl, J. M. *An Introduction to the Study of the Book of Mormon.* Salt Lake City: Deseret News Press, 1927.

Smith, Daymon M. *The Abridging Works: The Epic and Historic Book of Mormon Arranged in Sequence of Composition.* N.p.: self-published, 2011.

Smith, Joseph, trans. *The Book of Mormon: Another Testament of Jesus Christ.* New York: Doubleday, 2004.

———, trans. *The Book of Mormon.* Liverpool: William Budge, 1879.

———, trans. *The Book of Mormon.* Salt Lake City: The Church of Jesus Christ of Latter-day Saints, 1920.

Sperry, Sidney B. "The Book of Mormon as Translation English." *Journal of Book of Mormon Studies* 4, no. 1 (1995): 209–17.

———. *Book of Mormon Compendium.* Salt Lake City: Bookcraft, 1968.

Steinberg, Avi. *The Lost Book of Mormon: A Journey through the Mythic Lands of Nephi, Zarahemla, and Kansas City, Missouri.* New York: Doubleday, 2014.

Thayne, Stanley J. "'We're Going to Take Our Land Back Over': Indigenous Positionality, the Ethnography of Reading, and *The Book of Mormon*." In *Americanist Approaches to "The Book of Mormon,"* edited by Elizabeth Fenton and Jared Hickman, 321–38. New York: Oxford University Press, 2019.

Turley, Kylie Nielson. "Alma's Hell: Repentance, Consequence, and the Lake of Fire and Brimstone." *Journal of Book of Mormon Studies* 28 (2019): 1–45.

Turley, Richard E., Jr. *Victims: The LDS Church and the Mark Hofmann Case*. Urbana: University of Illinois Press, 1992.

Tvedtnes, John A. *The Isaiah Variants in the Book of Mormon*. Provo, UT: FARMS, 1981.

Van Wagoner, Richard, and Steve Walker. "Joseph Smith: 'The Gift of Seeing.'" *Dialogue: A Journal of Mormon Thought* 15, no. 2 (Summer 1982): 48–68.

Vogel, Dan. *Indian Origins and the Book of Mormon*. Salt Lake City: Signature Books, 1986.

———, ed. *The Word of God: Essays on Mormon Scripture*. Salt Lake City: Signature Books, 1990.

Walker, Ronald W., David J. Whittaker, and James B. Allen. *Mormon History*. Urbana: University of Illinois Press, 2001.

Welch, John W. "Chiasmus in the Book of Mormon." *BYU Studies* 10, no. 1 (1969): 69–84.

Welch, John W., and J. Gregory Welch. *Charting the Book of Mormon: Visual Aids for Personal Study and Teaching*. Provo, UT: FARMS, 1999.

Welch, Rosalynde. "Lehi's Brass Ball: Astonishment and Inscription." *Journal of Book of Mormon Studies* 29 (2020): 20–49.

West, Roy A. *An Introduction to the Book of Mormon: A Religious-Literary Study*. Salt Lake City: Department of Education of The Church of Jesus Christ of Latter-day Saints, 1940.

Westrup, Rebekah. "Imaginings of the Book of Mormon: A Comparison of Arnold Friberg's and Minerva Teichert's Book of Mormon Paintings." *Journal of Book of Mormon Studies* 29 (2020): 85–119.

White, O. Kendall, Jr. *Mormon Neo-orthodoxy: A Crisis Theology*. Salt Lake City: Signature Books, 1987.

Widtsoe, John A. *Joseph Smith: Seeker after Truth, Prophet of God*. Salt Lake City: Deseret News Press, 1951.

Index

A

academic charity, 76–77
amateur, 65
Americanist Approaches to "The Book of Mormon" (Fenton and Hickman), 45, 142
Analysis of Textual Variants of the Book of Mormon (Skousen), 132, 137
Ancient American Setting for the Book of Mormon, An (Sorenson), 21, 140, 151
Anderson, Lynn Matthews, 152
Anderson, Richard Lloyd, 32
"And He Was Anti-Christ" (Belnap), 146
"And It Came to Pass ..." (Belnap), 146
apologetics, faithful, 77–82
appendix, 131–63
   content in, 6–7
   essential works in Book of Mormon studies, 132–35
   institutions serving and supporting Book of Mormon studies, 153–57
   introduction to basic works in Book of Mormon studies, 135–42
   other sources cited, 158–63
   outline of works for specialization in Book of Mormon studies, 142–52
   questions answered in, 8
Arjuna, 50
Arnold, Marilyn, 19, 43, 148
Arrington, Leonard J., 17
Ashurst-McGee, Mark, 141
Association for Mormon Letters, 19, 28, 41
Austin, Michael, 44, 113

B

baptism, 58–59
Barlow, Philip L., 48, 49, 138, 142, 154
Beckwith, Francis J., 145

Index

"Becoming a People of the Books" (Johnson), 56, 138
Belnap, Daniel, 146, 147
Belnap, David M., 151
Benjamin, King, 120
Bennion, Francine R., 151
Benson, Ezra Taft, 19, 23, 28
Berkey, Kimberly Matheson, 53, 59–60, 152
Berrett, William E., 14
"Beyond Understanding" (Easton-Flake), 148
Bhagavad Gita, 50
Bible
   biblical scholarship, 149
   biblical theology, 51
   in contemporary Mormonism, 22
   early Latter-day Saint engagement with, 11–12, 55
   and intertextuality in Book of Mormon studies, 46–49, 80, 149–50
   literary criticism on, 40, 42
Bible, Mormon Scripture, and the Rhetoric of Allusivity, The (Frederick), 49, 142
biblical scholarship, 149
biblical theology, 51
Blythe, Christopher James, 56
Book of Mormon
   anachronisms in, 94–103
   antiquity of, 24–25
   changes made to, 88–91
   commentaries on, 71
   complexity of, 121–24
   criticism of, 14–15, 74, 111, 121–22
   defense of, 18–19, 20, 74–82, 122–23, 124
   as derived from nineteenth-century texts, 92–94
   and disability studies, 58–59, 117–18
   doctrinal study of, 23–24
   early Latter-day Saint engagement with, 11–12
   editions during Joseph Smith's lifetime, 88–89
   1879 edition of, 12–13, 66, 67–68
   familiarity with, 1–2, 12
   and gender issues, 58, 59–60, 75, 80, 116–17, 121, 151–52
   geography of, 103–6, 145–46
   grammar in, 90–91
   interpretation of, 73–74
   Isaiah in, 47, 97–100, 149–50
   literary criticism of, 40–45
   New Testament language in, 101–3
   original manuscript, 88
   and racial issues, 58, 59–60, 75, 114–16, 117, 121, 151
   readability of, 67–68
   reception and use of, 54–57, 134, 138–39, 149
   scholarship on historical origins of, 37–40, 41
   styles of writing about, 27
   textual production of, 31–36
   timeline of research on, 28
   translation of, 34–36, 84–88, 133
   treated as sacred fiction, 19–20
   as ubiquitous in Latter-day Saint life, 1
   uses and abuses of, 133–34
   warfare in, 118–19, 151
   women in, 116–17
Book of Mormon, The: A Biography (Gutjahr), 56, 133–34
Book of Mormon, The: Another Testament of Jesus Christ, Maxwell Institute Study Edition (Hardy), 67, 135–36
Book of Mormon, The: A Reader's Edition (Hardy), 136
Book of Mormon, The: A Very Short Introduction (Givens), 137
Book of Mormon, The: Brief Theological Introductions (Fluhman and Barlow), 54, 60, 71, 142, 154
Book of Mormon, The (Maffly-Kipp), 149
Book of Mormon, The: Second Nephi, the Doctrinal Structure (Nyman and Tate), 141

Book of Mormon, The: The Earliest Text (Skousen), 132–33, 137
Book of Mormon Academy, 157
"*Book of Mormon* as Amerindian Apocalypse, *The*" (Hickman), 45, 59
"Book of Mormon as a Modern Expansion of an Ancient Source, The" (Ostler), 141
"Book of Mormon as Post-Canonical Scripture, The" (Hardy), 50, 150
Book of Mormon Central, 69, 111, 156
Book of Mormon Critical Text (Smith), 143
Book of Mormon for the Least of These, The (Salleh and Hemming), 61–62, 150
"Book of Mormon Geographies" (Hedges), 145
Book of Mormon Reference Companion (Largey), 136–37
Book of Mormon studies, 2–5. *See also* Book of Mormon studies, common questions in; Book of Mormon studies, new directions in
   and antiquity of Book of Mormon, 24–25
   beginnings of, 11–13
   call for new vocabulary in, 76
   changes in, 63–64, 74, 127–28
   collaboration between believers and nonbelievers in, 109–10
   and doctrinal study of Book of Mormon, 23–24
   in early twentieth century, 13–15
   essential works in, 132–35
   and Foundation for Ancient Research and Mormon Studies, 18–30
   founding of, as academic discipline, 15–17
   future of, 124–25
   and Givens's *By the Hand of Mormon*, 25–27
   Hardy and, 27–29
   historical origins of Book of Mormon, 37–40, 41
   ideology critique in, 57–62
   and increased criticism of Church, 17–18
   institutions serving and supporting, 153–57
   intertextuality in, 46–50, 149–50
   introduction to basic works in, 135–42
   and Latter-day Saint intellectual movement, 17
   literary criticism in, 40–45
   obstacles facing, 64–82
   outline of works for specialization in, 142–52
   reception history in, 54–57, 134, 138–39, 149
   retooled, diversifying subdisciplines within, 75–76
   and textual production of Book of Mormon, 31–36
   theological interpretation in, 51–54, 152
   timeline of, 28
Book of Mormon studies, common questions in, 83–84, 106–7
   regarding anachronisms in Book of Mormon, 94–103
   regarding Book of Mormon geography, 103–6, 145–46
   regarding Book of Mormon translation, 84–88
   regarding changes to Book of Mormon text, 88–91
   regarding Isaiah in Book of Mormon, 97–100
   regarding New Testament language in Book of Mormon, 101–3
   regarding source of Book of Mormon, 92–94
Book of Mormon studies, new directions in, 109–14
   questions of identity, 114–18
   questions of meaning, 120–25

Index

Book of Mormon studies, new directions in (*continued*)
    questions of politics, 118–20, 150–51
Book of Mormon Studies Association, 156
Book of Mormon Symposium, 23, 147
Book of Mormon Testifies, The (Sperry), 144
"Book of Mormon Usage in Early LDS Theology" (Underwood), 55, 138
Bowman, Matthew, 152
Boxer, Elise, 61
Bradley, Don, 33, 72, 141
Brodie, Fawn McKay, 14–15, 25, 28, 32, 37, 41, 93, 139, 143
Brooke, John L., 33, 143
brother of Jared, 50
Brown, Samuel Morris, 144
Buddhism, 50
Bushman, Richard L., 32–33, 139, 143
By the Hand of Mormon (Givens), 25–27, 55–56, 134
BYU Religious Studies Center, 154–55
BYU Studies Quarterly, 153

C

Carmack, Stanford, 91
change, in Book of Mormon studies, 63–64, 74
charity, 76–77
Charlesworth, James H., 48, 140
chiasmus, 42, 140
"Chiasmus in the Book of Mormon" (Welch), 140
"Christ and Krishna" (Spencer), 50, 150
Christology, 123–24
Church of Jesus Christ of Latter-day Saints, The
    early engagement with Bible, 11–12, 55
    increased criticism of, 17–18
    Latter-day Saint history, 2

Latter-day Saint intellectual movement, 17
Latter-day Saint studies, 2
Coming Forth of the Book of Mormon, The (Largey et al.), 147
"Coming Forth of the Book of Mormon in the Twentieth Century, The" (Reynolds), 55, 138
common questions in Book of Mormon studies. *See* Book of Mormon studies, common questions in
Complete Concordance to the Book of Mormon, A (Reynolds), 13, 68
Compton, Todd M., 61
Coviello, Peter, 59, 148
Cowdery, Oliver, 88, 89
Cumorah, 104, 105

D

Davis, D. Morgan, 50
Davis, William L., 143–44
Demos, Rosemary, 152
dialogic revelation, 26
Dialogue: A Journal of Mormon Thought, 153–54
Dictionary of the Book of Mormon, A (Reynolds), 68
Digging in Cumorah (Thomas), 43, 148
Dirkmaat, Gerrit J., 33, 133
disability studies, 58–59, 117–18, 150
"Disability Studies Reading of Moroni Chapter 8, A" (Hodges), 58–59, 150
Doctrinal Commentary on the Book of Mormon (McConkie et al.), 52, 147
Doctrinal New Testament Commentary (McConkie), 51–52
doctrinal scholarship, 51–53
Documentary History of the Book of Mormon, A (Morris), 69, 143
"Does the Shoe Fit?" (Matheny), 146

Index

E

Early Mormonism and the Magic World View (Quinn), 33, 139
Easton-Flake, Amy, 56, 148, 152
"'East Wind,' An" (Hull), 146
Echoes and Evidences of the Book of Mormon (Parry et al.), 29, 137
England, Eugene, 19, 58, 151
Ericson, Loyd Isao, 145
Exploring the Book of Mormon in America's Heartland (Meldrum), 146

F

faithful apologetics, 77–82
Farrell, Heather, 152
Faulconer, James E., 19, 43, 52, 121
Feasting on the Word (Rust), 43, 148
Fenton, Elizabeth, 44–45, 94, 142, 148
Fluhman, J. Spencer, 142, 154
Foundation for Ancient Research and Mormon Studies (FARMS), 18–30
  and Book of Mormon translation, 35, 36
  critical responses to scholarship of, 145
  historically oriented scholarship of, 38–39
  and intertextuality in Book of Mormon studies, 48
  reference works published by, 68, 140–41, 144, 154
  and warfare in Book of Mormon, 118
  website of, 156
Frederick, Nicholas J., 49, 53, 141, 142, 147, 150
From Darkness unto Light (MacKay, Dirkmaat), 33, 133

G

Gardner, Brant A., 36, 39–40, 41, 71, 136, 143, 145
gender issues, 58, 59–60, 75, 80, 116–17, 121, 151–52
Geography of Book of Mormon Events, The (Sorenson), 145
Gift and Power, The (Gardner), 143
Gilbert, John, 88–89
Give Ear to My Words (Hull et al.), 147
Givens, Terryl L., 12, 25–27, 29, 55–56, 110–11, 134, 137
Goff, Alan, 43
Gore, David Charles, 53, 151
grammar, in Book of Mormon, 90–91
Granth, Adi, 50
"Great Cause to Mourn" (Berkey and Spencer), 59–60
Green, Deidre, 60, 152
Greg Kofford Books, 155
Groundwork: Studies in Theory and Scripture series, 154
Gutjahr, Paul C., 56, 133–34

H

Hamblin, William J., 151
Hardy, Grant
  The Book of Mormon: Another Testament of Jesus Christ, Maxwell Institute Study Edition, 67, 135–36
  The Book of Mormon: A Reader's Edition, 136
  "The Book of Mormon as Post-Canonical Scripture," 50, 150
  on complexity of Book of Mormon, 123
  on Isaiah in Book of Mormon, 100
  on Royal Skousen, 70
  scholarship of, 27–29
  "Speaking So That All May Be Edified," 148

Index

Hardy, Grant (*continued*)
  Understanding the Book of Mormon, 39–40, 43–44, 48–49, 72, 134–35
Hatem, Jad, 50, 53, 142
Hauglid, Brian M., 141
Hawkins, Lisa Bolin, 150–51
Hayes, John H., 149
"Heartland as Hinterland" (Wright), 146
Heartland model of Book of Mormon, 105–6, 146
Hedges, Andrew H., 145, 147
Hemming, Margaret Olsen, 59, 61–62, 150
Hickman, Jared, 45, 59, 142
Hill Cumorah, 104, 105
Hilton, John, III, 147
Hinduism, 49–50
History of the Text of the Book of Mormon, The (Skousen), 132, 143
Hodges, Blair Dee, 58–59, 150
Hofmann, Mark, 17, 19, 28
Holladay, Carl R., 149
Holland, David F., 148
How We Got the Book of Mormon (Turley and Slaughter), 136
Hull, Kerry, 41, 106, 146, 147
Hunt, Gilbert, 92, 93–94
Hunter, Milton R., 14
Hurd, Jerrie W., 151

I

identity, and new directions in Book of Mormon studies, 114–18
ideology critique, 57–62
infant baptism, 58–59
intellectual movement, Latter-day Saint, 17
Interpreter: A Journal of Latter-day Saint Faith and Scholarship, 153
intertextuality, 46–50, 80, 149–50
Introvigne, Massimo, 22

Isaiah, 47, 97–100, 149–50
Isaiah in the Book of Mormon (Parry and Welch), 144
Islam, 49–50

J

Jackson, Kent P., 148, 149
Jakeman, M. Wells, 15–16, 21, 25, 28, 37–38, 41, 65, 104
Jared, brother of, 50
Jensen, Robin Scott, 143
Johnson, Janiece, 56, 138
Johnson, Stanley A., 147
Jorgensen, Bruce W., 19, 41
"Joseph Smith and Native American Artifacts" (Wright), 145–46
Joseph Smith and the Beginnings of Mormonism (Bushman), 32–33, 143
Joseph Smith Papers, 68–69
Joseph Smith: Rough Stone Rolling (Bushman), 33, 139
Joseph Smith's Seer Stones (MacKay and Frederick), 141
Joseph Smith's Translation (Brown), 144
Joseph Smith: The Making of a Prophet (Vogel), 139
Journal of Book of Mormon Studies, 8, 21, 23, 29, 44, 50, 60, 137–38, 153, 154

K

King, Farina, 61
King Benjamin's Speech (Welch and Ricks), 140

L

Lambert, Neal E., 147–48
Largey, Dennis L., 69, 136–37, 147
Late War between the United States and Great Britain, The (Hunt), 92, 93–94

Index

Latter-day Saint history, 2
Latter-day Saint intellectual movement, 17
Latter-day Saint studies, 2
Latter-day Saint Theology Seminar, 52–53, 54, 156, 157
"Law of God/God of Law" (Shannon), 146–47
Legal Cases in the Book of Mormon, The (Welch), 144
literary criticism, 40–45
"loose control" model of Book of Mormon translation, 85–86, 90, 102
Lost 116 Pages, The: Reconstructing the Book of Mormon's Missing Stories (Bradley), 33, 72, 141

M

MacKay, Michael Hubbard, 33, 133, 141
Madsen, Truman G., 47–48
Maffly-Kipp, Laurie F., 149
Mason, Patrick Q., 61, 119, 151
Matheny, Deanne G., 146
Mauro, Hayes Peter, 61
Maxwell, Neal A., 80
Maxwell Institute, 156–57
McConkie, Bruce R., 51–52
McConkie, Joseph Fielding, 52, 147
Mead, James K., 149
meaning, and new directions in Book of Mormon studies, 120–25
Meldrum, Rod L., 146
mental health issues, 117–18. *See also* disability studies
Mesoamerican model of Book of Mormon, 104–5, 145–46
"Messianism in the Pseudepigrapha and the Book of Mormon" (Charlesworth), 140
Metcalfe, Brent Lee, 21–22, 38, 42–43, 145
Midgley, Louis, 23–24, 147

Miller, Adam S., 53, 152
Millet, Robert L., 23, 52, 147
Mitchell, Samuel, 44
Mormons and the Bible (Barlow), 48, 138
"Mormon Scholarship, Apologetics, and Evangelical Neglect" (Mosser and Owen), 145
Mormon's Codex (Sorenson), 145
Mormon studies, 2
Morris, Larry E., 69, 143
Mosser, Carl, 24, 145
Mueller, Max Perry, 151

N

Nelson, Russell M., 115
neo-orthodoxy / neo-orthodox moment, 51, 52
New Approaches to the Book of Mormon (Metcalfe), 21–22, 38, 42–43, 145
New Mormon Challenge, The (Beckwith et al.), 145
New Testament language, in Book of Mormon, 101–3
Nibley, Hugh
  apologetic work of, 79
  on Book of Mormon translation, 88
  on coming forth of Book of Mormon, 32, 35
  as FARMS scholar, 20–21
  on historicity of Book of Mormon, 25, 37–38, 41
  and ideology critique, 58
  and intertextuality in Book of Mormon studies, 47
  and literary criticism of Book of Mormon, 40
  No, Ma'am, That's Not History, 32, 143
  and shaping of Book of Mormon studies, 15–17, 28, 65
  Since Cumorah, 139
  specialized scholarship by, 144

Index

Nichols, Robert E., 19
No, Ma'am, That's Not History (Nibley), 32, 143
No Man Knows My History: The Life of Joseph Smith (Brodie), 14–15, 32, 37, 139
Nyman, Monte S., 141

O

obstacles, facing Book of Mormon studies, 64–82
"Open Canons" (Fenton), 44–45
Ostler, Blake T., 35–36, 141
Other Testament, An: On Typology (Spencer), 53, 72, 142
Our Book of Mormon (Sperry), 40, 139
Owen, Paul, 24, 145

P

Parry, Donald W., 137, 144
Pearson, Carol Lynn, 152
Pentecostal Reads the Book of Mormon, A (Thomas), 142
Perry, Seth, 148
Peterson, Daniel C., 137
Phelps, W. W., 51
politics, and new directions in Book of Mormon studies, 118–20, 150–51
Porter, Bruce H., 146
Postponing Heaven (Hatem), 50, 53, 142
poverty, 120
Pratt, Orson, 12–13, 28, 51, 65, 66, 67–68
Problems of the Book of Mormon, The (Sperry), 144
Producing Ancient Scripture (MacKay et al.), 141
Prophecies and Promises (Porter and Meldrum), 146
"Prophetic Messages or Dogmatic Theology?" (Midgley), 147

"Prophets and Prophecy in the Qur'an and the Book of Mormon" (Davis), 50
prosperity, 120
Pulsipher, J. David, 56, 61, 119, 151

Q

questions. *See* Book of Mormon studies, common questions in
Quinn, D. Michael, 33, 139
Qur'an, 50

R

racial issues, 58, 59–60, 75, 114–16, 117, 121, 151
reception history, 54–57, 134, 138–39, 149
Refiner's Fire, The (Brooke), 33, 143
Religious Educator: Perspectives on the Restored Gospel, 153
Religious Studies Center, 154–55
religious texts, and intertextuality in Book of Mormon studies, 49–50, 150
Restoration, study of, 17
Revelations and Translations, Volume 3 (Skousen and Jensen), 143
Revelations and Translations, Volume 5 (Skousen and Jensen), 143
Reynolds, George, 13, 28, 65, 67–68, 69–71
Reynolds, Noel B., 40–41, 55, 138, 144, 149
Reynolds, Philip C., 70
rhetorical authority, 102
Ricks, Stephen D., 140, 151
Roberts, B. H., 13, 14, 28, 34, 35, 65, 71–72, 92
Robinson, Ebenezer, 89
Robinson, Stephen E., 23
Rust, Richard Dilworth, 19, 22, 41, 43, 148

S

Salleh, Fatimah, 59, 61–62, 150
Sawyer, John F. A., 149
Second Witness (Gardner), 39, 71, 136
Seely, David Rolph, 144
Seely, Jo Ann H., 144
Sermon at the Temple and the Sermon on the Mount, The (Welch), 144
Sermon on the Mount, 48
"Sermon on the Mount and Third Nephi, The" (Stendahl), 140
Shalev, Eran, 94, 148
Shannon, Avram R., 146–47
Sidney B. Sperry Symposium, 147, 154
Signature Books, 21–23, 28, 38–39, 48, 155
Since Cumorah (Nibley), 139
Sjödahl, Janne M., 13–14, 28, 65, 69–71, 149
Skinner, Andrew C., 144
Skousen, Royal
  analysis of Book of Mormon print history, 66–67, 68
  Analysis of Textual Variants of the Book of Mormon, 132, 137
  The Book of Mormon: The Earliest Text, 132–33, 137
  on Book of Mormon translation, 36
  on grammar in Book of Mormon, 91
  The History of the Text of the Book of Mormon, 132, 143
  Revelations and Translations, Volume 3, 143
  Revelations and Translations, Volume 5, 143
  significance in Book of Mormon studies, 70
  "Translating the Book of Mormon," 141
Slaughter, William W., 136
Smith, Daymon M., 149
Smith, Don Carlos, 89
Smith, Ethan, 92–94

Smith, Gregory L., 146
Smith, Hank R., 147
Smith, Joseph
  and Book of Mormon translation, 34–36, 84–88
  and coming forth of Book of Mormon, 14–15, 32, 111
  and historicity of Book of Mormon, 26
  and origins of Book of Mormon, 92–94
  and revisions made to Book of Mormon, 88–91
Smith, Robert, 66, 143
Snow, Edgar, 43
Sondrup, Steven P., 19, 41
Sorenson, John L., 16, 21, 22, 38, 41, 58, 104, 140, 145, 151
Spaulding manuscript, 92, 93
"Speaking So That All May Be Edified" (Hardy), 148
Spencer, Joseph M., 49, 50, 53, 59–60, 72, 142, 150, 152
Sperry, Sidney B., 15–17, 21, 25, 28, 34, 40, 47, 65, 139, 144. *See also* Sidney B. Sperry Symposium
Sproat, Ethan, 151
Stendahl, Krister, 48, 140
Story of the Book of Mormon, The (Reynolds), 13
Strathearn, Gaye, 144, 147
Sunstone, 153–54
Sweet Is the Word (Arnold), 43, 148

T

Talmage, James E., 14, 28
Tate, Charles D., Jr., 141, 149
Tate, George S., 41
textual production, 31–36
Thayne, Stanley J., 61
theological interpretation, 51–54, 152
theology, 51, 53
Things Which My Father Saw, The (Belnap et al.), 147

Index

Thomas, John Christopher, 53, 142
Thomas, Mark D., 19, 22–23, 27, 41, 43, 148
Thomas, Robert K., 19
Thomasson, Gordon C., 150–51
Three Nephites, 50
"tight control" model of Book of Mormon translation, 85–86, 90–91
tone, and academic charity, 76
Top, Brent L., 147
Traditions of the Fathers (Gardner), 145
transcontinental railroad, 127
"Translating the Book of Mormon" (Skousen), 141
Turley, Kylie, 44
Turley, Richard E., Jr., 136
Twain, Mark, 101, 123

U

Understanding the Book of Mormon (Hardy), 39–40, 43–44, 48–49, 72, 134–35
Underwood, Grant, 55, 138
undogmatic, 73

V

Van Dyke, Blair G., 145
Van Wagoner, Richard, 35
View of the Hebrews (Smith), 92–94
violence, 61. See also warfare
Vision of All, The (Spencer), 49
Visions in a Seer Stone (Davis), 143–44
Vogel, Dan, 38, 139

W

Walker, Steven C., 19, 35
warfare, 118–19, 151. See also violence
Webb, Jenny, 152
websites, 155–56
Welch, John W., 21, 22, 38, 40–41, 137, 140, 144
Welch, Rosalynde Frandsen, 53

"We're Going to Take Our Land Back Over" (Thayne), 61
West, Roy A., 14
Westrup, Rebekah, 57
White, O. Kendall, Jr., 51
Widtsoe, John A., 34
Williams, Camille S., 152
Williams, Mandy Jane, 152
women, in Book of Mormon, 116–17. See also gender issues
world scripture, 49–50, 150
Wright, Mark, 41, 145–46

Z

Zion, 75–76

About the Authors

Daniel Becerra is an assistant professor of ancient scripture at Brigham Young University and is a scholar of early Christianity. He received a PhD in religion (early Christianity) and an MA in religious studies from Duke University, an MTS in New Testament/early Christianity from Harvard Divinity School, and a BA in ancient Near Eastern studies from Brigham Young University. His primary research interests concern moral formation in late antiquity (ca. 2nd–7th centuries CE), particularly within Christian ascetic contexts. His published works on the Book of Mormon include *3rd, 4th Nephi: A Brief Theological Introduction*.

Amy Easton-Flake received her PhD in American literature, with an emphasis in nineteenth-century women's literature and narrative theory, from Brandeis University in 2011. She also received an MA in women's studies from Brandeis, an MA in English from Brigham Young University, and a BA in American studies and marriage, family, and human development from Brigham Young University. Her research interests include nineteenth-century women's reform literature, nineteenth-century women's biblical hermeneutics, Latter-day Saint "home literature" in relation to the larger print culture, the Book of Mormon through a narrative lens, and reception history of the Book of Mormon. She and her husband, Merrill, are the parents of two children.

Nicholas J. Frederick is an associate professor at Brigham Young University. He attended BYU, where he received his BA in classics and his MA in comparative studies. He then attended Claremont Graduate University, where he completed a PhD in the history of Christianity with an emphasis in Mormon studies, after which he returned to BYU to teach full-time in Religious Education. His research focuses primarily on the intertextual relationship between the text of the Bible and Latter-day Saint scripture, specifically the Book of Mormon. He has been married to Julie Parker Frederick for eighteen years and is the father of four children.

Joseph M. Spencer received a PhD in philosophy from the University of New Mexico before joining the faculty as an assistant professor of ancient scripture at Brigham Young University. He is the author of five books and many articles, and he serves as the editor of the *Journal of Book of Mormon Studies*, as the associate director of the Latter-day Saint Theology Seminar, and as a vice president (and founding member) of the Book of Mormon Studies Association. His research focuses on the point of connection between philosophy and scripture. He and his wife, Karen, live in Provo with their children.